BEHIND
CLOSED
DOORS

BEHIND CLOSED DOORS

Christians, Pornography, and the Temptations of Cyberspace

ROBERT J. BAIRD, M.DIV., MSW, PH.D.
RONALD L. VANDERBECK, PSY.D.

THE HOPE AND HEALING INSTITUTE

PUBLISHER'S NOTE: This book is intended for general information only and is not intended to supplant advice, diagnosis, treatment, or therapy by a personal physician or professional counselor.

Published in Grand Rapids, Michigan by the Hope and Healing Institute.

Scripture quotations marked NIV are taken from the HOLY BIBLE: NEW INTERNATIONAL VERSION®, copyright © 1973, 1978, 1984 by the International Bible Society, used by permission of Zondervan Publishing House. All rights reserved.

Printed in the United States of America.

ISBN-13:   978-0-9799456-0-1

In an age when children and families are at risk of being affected by destructive forms of sexuality and the distortions of pornography, The *Hope and Healing Institute* is a non-denominational ministry committed to a ministry of healing, protection and renewal. The Institute provides an extensive range of services including crisis intervention, clinical counseling, psychological assessment, forensic consultation, and life coaching. The Institute is dedicated to bring hope and healing to those who are hurting due to problems associated with pornography, cybersex, sexual abuse, incest, infidelity, and sexual addiction.

The Institute's executive directors, board, and staff are committed to a global initiative to protect children and families from the dangers of the Internet and other forms of destructive sexuality. The Institute has one fundamental goal: to unite the worldwide faith community to be more proactive in combating the proliferation of pornography and the exploitation of children, adolescents, and adults.

The Institute is a sanctuary of solace and healing for those who have been victimized and a place where strugglers experience the redemptive grace of Jesus Christ.

For more information, please visit www.hopeandhealinginstitute.com

Contents

"Here I am! I stand at the door and knock."

REVELATION 3:20, NIV

An Invitation to Renewal and Restoration

Tim's wife had only been gone for a minute or so. As usual he had given her a peck on the cheek, wished her a good day, and waved goodbye. He waited until she had pulled her car out of the driveway before he booted up his computer. Ever since he'd gotten his new computer he looked forward to her leaving for work. It's not that he didn't love her; he truly did. But this was time for him to do something he wouldn't conceive of doing when she was at home. He closed the door to the den and removed from his chair the notes he had brought home from last night's Bible study. It didn't take him long to get comfortable and to find what he was looking for. He had his favorite sites. Within moments he was so immersed in what he was doing that he never heard the door open. His heartbroken wife stood speechless.

John graduated toward the top of his class in law school and was quickly recruited by a prestigious firm. With a private office, personal secretary, and law clerks to assist him, he was given all the resources to be a successful attorney. However, the senior partners could not understand why his billings were so low. He always arrived early and was one of the last to leave. But John wasn't working on briefs when he was behind the closed doors of his office.

Kate considered herself a typical soccer mom. Her husband had a good paying job, so she didn't have to work. She had three kids whom she would cart around to school and sporting events. By all appearances she seemed to have the perfect life. Nice husband. Great kids. Big house. But Kate was bored. Her husband spent so many hours at work that she didn't feel her needs were being met. So Kate turned to Internet chatrooms. She wasn't looking primarily for sex. What she craved was affirmation and affection. There, she found the attention she sought.

Stephen was a sophomore in high school. His parents took him to see a psychologist who specializes in adolescent depression. And for sure, Stephen presented with all the telltale signs of depression. He was sleeping through all of his classes at school. He was no longer hanging out with his friends. He used to be an avid soccer player, but not any more. Clinically speaking, he was depressed. But what his parents didn't know was that after they went to bed at night, Stephen would quietly boot up his computer and surf through porn sites till the wee hours of the morning.

Jill was in middle school—eighth grade, to be exact. When her parents came to the offices of The Hope and Healing Institute, both of their faces were ashen. Her father's hands trembled as he described their discovery of pictures on their daughter's digital camera, pictures of Jill and her boyfriend. They had met in their church's youth group. What should have been a story of puppy love instead escalated to become a story of coercion. The boyfriend had introduced Jill to the world of "virtual" reality, where reality quickly becomes distorted. Jill truly believed that what she encountered there represented normal relationships. But she had nothing to base her conclusion on since sex was never openly discussed in her home.

If any of these stories sounds familiar to you, it's not surprising. Statistics show that one in five Americans uses the Internet to look for pornography or engage in cybersexual "chat." In fact, sex is the most frequently searched topic on the Internet— more than games, music, travel, jokes, cars, jobs, weather, and health material *combined*.[1] In a recent survey, one in ten people reported believing he or she was addicted to sex via the Internet. Moreover, one in four disclosed feeling that on at least one occasion his or her online sexual behavior was out of control.[2]

Focus on the Family conducted a survey with Zogby International indicating that one out of five American adults may have looked for sex on the Internet. Twenty percent of the respondents admitted to having visited a sexually oriented website (representing approximately 40 million adults). In this survey nearly 26 percent of men and nearly 17 percent of women indicated that it was either somewhat or very likely that the Internet is capable of providing sexual fulfillment. Not sexual stimulation; sexual fulfillment.[3]

Rabbit Hunting and the Proliferation of Porn

In 1953 an event took place that would forever change the moral complexion of American society: the publication of *Playboy* magazine. With his bunny insignia and Playboy Playmates, Hugh Hefner introduced pornography into mainstream American culture. What before had been shunned or ridiculed was soon to become not only tolerated but also celebrated. Prior to *Playboy*, the public perception was that users of porn were perverted or twisted. But Hefner marketed his material in such a way that his readers could consider themselves sophisticated, intelligent, and debonair. In a very real way pornography became fashionable. No longer hidden in back alleys, pornography became readily available at newsstands and delivered by the U.S. Postal Service.

The popularity of Hefner's product was enormous, and for nearly fifteen years Playboy Enterprises monopolized the market. Then, in 1969, an advertisement appeared in the *New York Times*. It featured *Playboy*'s bunny logo centered in a rifle sight accompanied by the caption, "We're going rabbit hunting." The ad went on to read, "If you can catch a rabbit once you can catch him again. That's what we did in Germany and France. The U.S. market will be the next to fall. We are going to catch this rabbit in his own backyard. We are the magazine that gives men what they are looking for."

And so began the pornography wars. *Penthouse* declared a full offensive in attempt to dominate the market. In 1974 Larry Flynt joined the fray, launching *Hustler* magazine. As these publishers pressed to achieve a larger share of the market, they pushed the envelope of acceptability. In a short period of time, the images depicted in these magazines changed from erotica to full frontal nudity. Over the next twenty years, content of these publications would include ever-increasingly hardcore sexual depictions.

The technology of the 1970s and 1980s then catapulted pornography into a multi-billion dollar industry. Cable and satellite TV permitted viewers to access pornography from the privacy of their homes. No longer was there a risk of being seen purchasing a dirty magazine. Behind closed doors Americans were beginning to do in private what they never would have considered doing in public.

The introduction of VHS tapes and inexpensive videocassette players magnified the problem. In 1978, 100 hard-core films were released. In 1996, that number climbed to 8,000. In 2002, over 11,000 hard-core films were released, compared with 470 Hollywood features. Hardcore video rentals increased from $75 million annually in 1985 to $490 million in 1992, and to $665 million in 1996.[4] What happened next, though, makes these statistics seem miniscule by comparison.

The introduction of the Internet in the 1990s granted anyone with a personal computer and Internet connection access to pornography twenty-four hours a day, seven days a week. With little to no restrictions, people of all ages now have access to a vast smorgasbord of smut. All it takes is the click of a mouse to view all sorts of images, from the erotic and titillating to the downright bizarre.

The Reality of Internet Pornography

- According to the Internet Filter Review, worldwide pornography revenue in 2006 was $97.06 billion. They estimate that there are 4.2 million pornographic websites, 420 million pornographic webpages, and 68 million daily pornographic search engine requests.

- According to Media Metrix, Internet users viewed over 15 billion pages of adult content in a single month.

- Child pornography is one of the fastest growing businesses online, and the content is becoming worse. In 2004, the Internet Watch Foundation found 3,433 child abuse domains; in 2006, they identified 10,656 child abuse domains.

- Worldwide revenue from mobile phone pornography is expected to rise to $1 billion and could grow to three times that number or more within a few years.

- In research conducted by the Polly Klaas Foundation, almost one in eight youth ages 8-18 discovered that someone they were communicating with online was an adult pretending to be much younger.

- 42% of Internet users aged 10 to 17 had seen online pornography in a recent 12-month span. Of those, 66% said they did not want to view the images and had not sought them out.

- Sex is the #1 searched for topic on the Internet.

- 60% of all website visits are sexual in nature.

- According to *Today's Christian Woman*, one out of every six women, including Christians, struggles with pornography.

- 51% of pastors say cyberporn is a possible temptation. 37% say it is a current struggle. 4 in 10 pastors have visited a porn site.

Data provided by Enough Is Enough[5]

An Invitation
to Renewal and Restoration

No question about it, an astonishing number of people within the faith community struggle with sexual sin on the Internet. And it is for them, their spouses, and others who want to help them that this book is written. This book, however, is not just about calling attention to a problem. This book is about solutions. With inspiration from Scripture and insight from the behavioral sciences, this book presents specific and practical interventions to assist those struggling with sexual sin stemming from the Internet. The purpose of this book is to liberate people from sexual sin not only by educating them to the risks and destructive power of cybersexual behavior, but also to provide the tools and strategies essential for life-changing renewal and transformation.

The format of this book is essentially the same for each chapter. Beginning with personal stories based on the experiences of those who sought treatment at the Hope and Healing Institute, each chapter then provides an analysis of the situation as well as encouraging biblical references intended to inspire hope. Most importantly readers will find practical strategies designed to help renew and restore a healthy, Christian sexuality.

Our hope is that you'll discover the solution to recovery is a renewed relationship with God. Throughout these chapters may his gentle call inspire changed thoughts and behaviors and a new way of living as followers of Christ.

Sexual struggles are not new. As accounted for in the Bible, humanity has struggled with sexual issues throughout the ages. Joseph encountered sexual temptation when Potiphar's wife tried to seduce him (Gen.39:7-19). Sexual gluttony contributed to the destruction of Sodom and Gomorrah (Gen.18:16-33). Lot and his two daughters had an incestuous relationship (Gen. 19:30-38). Abraham believed his wife was incapable of conceiving a child, so he chose to have an adulterous relationship with Hagar (Gen. 16:1-16). Believing she was a prostitute, Judah slept with his daughter-in-law (Gen. 38). Sexual manipulation is implied in the story of Samson and Delilah (Judg. 16). The King of Israel, David, abused his power in order to have an adulterous affair with Bathsheba (2 Sam. 11-12). David's third son, Absalom, rebelled against his father and made it public knowledge that he had sexual relations with all of his father's wives (2 Sam. 18:6-15).

Warnings against adultery are specified in Prov. 6:20-29. The destructiveness of adultery is addressed, metaphorically, in the *Allegory of Unfaithful Jerusalem* (Ezek. 16). In his letter to the church in Rome, the Apostle Paul addressed the multiplicity of ways in which people rebel against a covenant relationship with God, including sexual immorality. Similar admonitions appear in another letter penned by Paul, this one to the church located in one of the largest seaports—Corinth—in the Roman Empire, a city renowned for sexual excesses and immorality. In 1 Corinthians 5, Paul insists that such practices not be tolerated in the church.

The Bible, in many ways, is a book about relationships. The Bible is about people's relationship with God and with each other. What is remarkable about the stories contained in the Bible is how real they are. As a book that serves as the foundation of an entire faith system, it's remarkable how genuine and authentic these stories are. The superheroes of our faith, our Biblical ancestors, had problems similar to ours. Like Christians in the twenty-first century, they struggled with temptation. Like Christians whose lives are surrounded by a secular, sexualized culture, they too made bad choices.

But the stories in the Bible are also stories of redemption. And so are the stories you are about to read in this book. These are stories of people from the faith community who experienced the dark, chaotic forces of cyberspace. As clients who sought treatment at the Hope and Healing Institute, they have agreed to share their stories. Only names and other identifying information have been changed to protect their privacy.

One of their stories may be your story. Our prayer is that, by the grace of God, you too will accept God's invitation to renewal and restoration.

"I Was Just Curious"

The Temptations of Internet Pornography

DAVE'S STORY

My name is Dave. For about three years, though, I might as well have been known as Dr. Jekyll or Mr. Hyde. I lived a secret life that was known only to me, a surreptitious existence contaminated by pornography.

Nobody knew about my dark side until the week after my wife threw a surprise birthday party to celebrate my fortieth birthday. She had invited practically everyone and anyone we had ever known. Family, my parents, friends, the pastor, and even my boss were invited. She and the kids put together a PowerPoint presentation detailing my life's journey. Most of it was humorous, but there were some photographs that served as a stark reminder of who I had been and what I had become.

After the presentation, there were speeches. My eldest son talked about me being the coach for just about every team sport my kids ever played. He poked fun at me, suggesting that I had wanted to relive my childhood (which was probably true). He talked about me always being at his teacher conferences and about the time when he was in the sixth grade school play and I cancelled a business trip just to be there. He mentioned how I was always pestering him and his brother and sister to do their homework and joked about "dad's alarm clock" that seemed to go off at the same time each night when I would make them go to their rooms to do their homework. Little did he know that I would send them off to their rooms so I could do some "work" of my own on the computer. My best friend gave a little speech poking fun at my receding hairline. His gift to me was a pair of bifocal reading glasses and some hair dye to cover up the gray. In his speech he talked about how he has never seen me lose my temper (except when the Yankees lost the World Series to the Diamondbacks). He called me a "family man" and praised me for my love and devotion to my wife and kids.

Later that night my wife commented that she thought it was sweet that I began blushing while he was speaking. What she didn't know was that the truth of what I'd been doing online made me feel like anything *but* a devoted husband and father. Following my best friend, my pastor spoke of my commitment to the church and my willingness to teach Sunday school and open our home for Bible study. It is true; for the past ten years I have volunteered to teach Sunday school. It's also true that for years my wife and I have hosted numerous Bible studies in our home. But what he didn't know— what no one knew— was that the same computer I used to write material for Christian education was also used to surf the World Wide Web for pornography.

The showering of praise and attention at my birthday party was more than I could bear. Later that night, after everyone was gone and my wife and I were lying in bed, I prayed and started to cry. I'm not a touchy-feely type of guy, and so tears are not typical for me, but the experience from that night cut me to the core. I realized I was no longer the person I wanted to be. I realized I was no longer the person I knew my wife wanted me to be. I realized I was no longer the man that Christ called me to be.

It took me a week to muster up the courage to talk to my wife, but I had to. I had to tell her what was going on and that I needed to make a radical change to get my life back in order.

I told her (just as I'm telling you) that pornography has not always been a problem for me. It was only over the span of three years that my life was turned upside-down because of that stuff. Back when I was a teenager as well as in college, I would occasionally look at my friends' *Playboy* magazines, but it was never something I did on a regular basis. I never bought a magazine or rented a video. Until the Internet came along, pornography had never been a problem.

For me, my troubles started out of curiosity.

We first connected to the Internet in the early '90s. At that time my motivation (and I say this with all sincerity) was good. I wanted my children to benefit educationally. The World Wide Web had so many positive benefits. The kids could do research for their homework, and my wife and I could email family and friends at any time. It was relatively cheap and fast. Since my parents were aging and struggling with health problems, I could use the Internet to find information on healthcare. It was fascinating how quickly I could find just about anything I wanted simply by clicking the mouse and typing in a few key words.

To say that my first encounter with Internet pornography was accidental would be a lie. I knew exactly what I was doing. I didn't know, though, what I was getting myself into. It was late at night and my wife and kids were in bed asleep. I turned the computer screen to the side, just in case my wife should walk in. I had heard all the talk about Internet porn and was curious to see what it was all about. That night, after connecting to the Internet, I typed in four letters: p-o-r-n. Within moments of hitting the Enter key, I had a long list of Web sites offering me an unimaginable array of choices. I hesitated for a moment— but no longer. I knew I shouldn't be doing it, but I clicked the mouse anyway. In that moment, my life took an unexpected turn.

What was I doing? I never was the kind of person who would go to stores and buy porn. That just seemed wrong and, besides, I'd rather die than be seen going into an adult bookstore! But here I was, on the Internet looking at porn sites. It was so private and secret. No one knew what I was doing, and there was so much to see. As

I surfed around, I wondered where on earth they found all of those attractive women to pose like that.

My first experience lasted about an hour that night, until the family dog walked into the room. I didn't even know she was there until she nudged the back of my chair. I nearly had a heart attack thinking it was my wife or one of the kids. I remember yanking the power cord right out of the wall. Startled by the dog, I momentarily came to my senses. In that moment, a wave of shame washed over me. What I'd been doing was wrong, and I knew it. The next morning my wife sensed that something was up, but I didn't dare tell her what I'd done. I promised myself that I would never do it again.

But, about a month later, the entire scenario repeated itself. Again, it was late at night and everyone had gone to bed. I concocted some excuse to tell my wife that I had to work on a project for my boss—the first of many lies. This time, however, I locked the door. I knew what I was doing was wrong, and I didn't want to get caught.

Once again, I went online to see what was there. What I found was beyond anything I could've ever imagined. There were pictures of women posing provocatively, and there were images of couples together in very explicit scenes. The content of the pictures ranged from erotic to hardcore. There were seemingly millions of pictures of eighteen- and nineteen-year-old girls. On occasion I would stumble upon something really disgusting, like people having sex with animals. But with the click of the mouse, I could quickly exit that Web site and surf onto something more appealing. It was a pornographic smorgasbord with some really appetizing stuff and some stuff I'd rather pass over. But that is what made the whole experience difficult to resist! I could surf from site to site in search of more tantalizing choices. If I happened upon something unappetizing, I could quickly bypass it. All the time I kept telling myself that at least I wasn't as bad as the guys who chose to look at the illegal and downright bizarre stuff.

In the beginning, I went porn-surfing only once in a while. Before long, however, I found myself looking forward to the times I could be alone on the computer. I found myself returning to some of the same sites. Sometimes I explored different sites. It all depended on how much time I had and my mood at the moment. I found the whole experience very arousing and exciting. I found myself making excuses for my behavior. If my wife wasn't "in the mood" or if I'd a hard day at work, I convinced myself that it was OK to go online. I realize now that these excuses only served to justify what I was doing. I knew it was wrong. But I was still drawn to it. And afterwards I would feel depressed and ashamed. I was too embarrassed to talk to anyone about what I was doing. How could I tell my pastor? How could I tell my best friend? How could I tell my wife? I was too ashamed to reveal my secret sin, but the guilt was overwhelming. I made countless promises to myself not to do it again. Sometimes I was successful, sometimes not. I could go for days and even weeks without looking. And when I slipped up, I prayed for forgiveness and the strength to change. But the temptation seemed too difficult to resist.

As time went on, I learned about chatrooms where people would "trade" pictures. The more I emailed pictures back and forth with people I didn't know, the more I came to believe that what I was doing wasn't all that bad. How could it be when I would chat with other guys online— other *Christian* guys—who also found this stuff nearly impossible to resist. Must be normal, right? Over time I began feeling less guilty and self-conscious about my activity because there were seemingly so many other guys doing the very same thing.

I'd convinced myself that what I was doing wasn't hurting anyone and that it wasn't affecting me or my family. But I was wrong. For starters, it affected my sexual relationship with my wife. Online I would see pictures and video clips of women and couples doing things that I wanted to re-enact with my wife. I found myself wanting sex with her more often and getting frustrated that she wasn't responding the way the women did online. They wanted it all the time and could never get enough. But my wife seemed satisfied with making love once a week. I started thinking that something must be wrong with her. But it was me. My thoughts, my expectations were being warped by what I was seeing online.

My porn use also affected my relationships with my children. While I never fully abandoned them, I do know that I missed out on an awful lot these past three years. Soon they will be off to college and our nest will be empty. And for the rest of my life I will regret what could have been.

Most importantly, my use of Internet porn affected my relationship with God. I can honestly say that over these past three years I saw a gradual decline in the amount of time I spent in prayer and devotions. Before my addiction escalated, I would go to worship and sing God's praises and totally concentrate on the pastor's message. But then things changed. I became more like a hollow shell. I was going through the motions, but never fully engaged. I was turning away from God. By failing to resist the temptation, my time, my energy, and my soul were lured away from my Lord.

And it all started out of simple curiosity.

Curiosity *Can* Kill the Cat

Most Christian men will admit, even if only to themselves, that sexual temptation confronts them on a daily basis. Living in an overly sexualized society, men are constantly bombarded with erotic and explicit images. Whether it's billboard advertising or commercials on TV, the swimsuit edition of *Sports Illustrated* or the *Victoria's Secret* catalogue, men constantly encounter images that capture their visual attention and tempt their souls. What makes these images so difficult to resist is that men are, by God's design, visual creatures. The male body is "wired" to respond emotionally and physically to something attractive.

In early adolescence, boys begin to realize the powerful draw of visual stimulation. Most men can recall sitting in a junior-high classroom, totally captivated by a girl they considered beautiful. It was infatuation, pure and simple, a response to visual stimulation. As young men begin to mature and develop emotionally, the visual attraction becomes coupled with a desire for emotional and relational intimacy resulting in courtships, expressions of love, and covenant vows of marriage. However, at their core, men remain wired to respond to visual stimuli. When exposed to pornography, there is a natural, physiological reaction. A *powerful* reaction. One that is hard to resist.

Many men struggle with the temptation to use the Internet to look at pornography. In a moment of weakness, some will look out of curiosity. They've heard all the rumors about the abundance of titillating images and think they'll "just take a peek" to check it out. Some may do just that and never repeat the indiscretion. Others, however, find themselves returning to the virtual world of cyberporn time and again. The reality is that nearly sixty percent of all visits to Web sites are sexual in nature. Twenty-five million Americans visit cybersex sites between 1-10 hours per week. Seventy percent of these people keep their behaviors secret.[2]

Those in the porn industry know full and well that their product is tempting and hard to resist. More than that, they are keenly aware of just how addictive pornography can be. In fact, their entire marketing strategy is built upon the reality that a person can become addicted. The approach taken by the porn industry is to distribute their product for free, doing so with the confidence that after a short while the user will become hooked and then begin to pay in order to access the material. By distributing their product for free, the industry manipulates and preys upon curiosity-seekers and those who succumb to temptation. As of July 2007 a websearch using Google with key words "free porn" generated 23 million webpages. Even though they offer much of their product for free, the pornography industry still manages to generate more than $97 billion in worldwide revenues.[3]

Dogs, Pigeons, and Computer Mice

Most of the clients who seek help at the Hope and Healing Institute describe how their problems with Internet pornography began out of curiosity. They all insist that they never would've considered going into an adult bookstore, but felt safe exploring pornography from the privacy of their own homes. With no one to see them and potentially expose and embarrass them, they felt safe to satisfy their curiosity behind closed doors.

Most clients tell similar stories of lives spiraling out of control. Of course, none of them intended for or even anticipated this consequence. In fact, many of them believed that they *were* in control. They were managing their cyberporn use. They were "just looking." But for each of them something happened that forced them to realize that, because of the porn, their lives were no longer manageable. Whether it was a spouse's discovery of their porn use, a child stumbling upon a surprising secret on the home computer, or disciplinary action by an employer for vio-

Risk Factors

There are three key factors that influence sexual expression and interaction on the Internet. Known as the Triple-A Model (as developed by Dr. Al Cooper, the Clinical Director at the San Jose Marital and Sexuality Center)[4], these conditions make people vulnerable to the powerful temptation to use the Internet to view pornography or engage in other cybersexual behavior:

Accessibility. The cold, stark reality is that pornography and cybersexual material is available twenty-four hours a day, seven days a week. You don't even need to leave the comfort of your home to access it.

lating the company's Internet-use policy, something happened which made them realize they had a big problem on their hands.

What had begun as simple curiosity had morphed into something far more sinister and problematic. The changes these people experienced were the result of a psychological phenomenon known as conditioning.

Anyone who's ever owned a cat or a dog knows the fundamental principle of conditioning, which was studied and documented by Russian scientist Ivar Pavlov. Pavlov conditioned his dogs to salivate whenever they heard a bell ring. He did this simply by ringing a bell any time he fed his dogs. Before long, the dogs began to salivate when they heard sound of the bell because they associated that sound with food. The mere ringing of the bell, even with no food in sight, was enough to get the dogs aroused.

Something similar happens to those who use their computers to access pornography and engage in cybersexual behavior. They begin to associate a computer and the Internet with sexual

Affordability. As mentioned above, there are more than 23 million pornography sites available free of charge. No credit card. No debit card. No contracts. No obligation. It's all free— until a sexual addiction compels the user to take out his American Express or Visa card.

Anonymity. From the privacy of their home or office, persons who surf the Internet for sexual material do so believing they're doing it anonymously. They log on to the Internet using screen names that cloak their identities. People enter virtual reality believing it's a vast masquerade ball.

stimulation. Whether it's the sound of the computer modem, the gentle hum of the computer fan, or clicks on the keyboard, people can become conditioned to associate these auditory stimulations with sexual arousal. Curiosity-seekers are unaware that their minds and bodies are being conditioned to associate the computer with pleasurable feelings of sexual arousal. The result is that their capacity to resist temptation erodes, placing them at risk of developing personal or relational problems, even cybersexual addiction.

Warning Signs

The following are warning signs that a person's use of the Internet has progressed from a momentary spiritual lapse (curiosity) to a something far more problematic:

A change in sleep habits. In a desire to not get "caught in the act," those using their computers to access pornography will do so only when they have privacy. In the context of marriage or family, such time can be limited. As a result, those whose curiosity becomes habit-forming will deliberately alter their sleep habits. Some will complain of insomnia. Others will claim a need "to get some work done on the computer" and come to bed later or rise earlier in the morning.

Moodiness and irritability. Although pornography can be physically stimulating, arousing, and pleasurable, most Christians who've fallen to the temptation of pornography are well aware that their behavior is unacceptable. This inner conflict often manifests itself in moodiness and irritability. When struggling with the burden of sexual temptation, those who are typically light-hearted and jovial can appear depressed and often develop a rather short-fused temper.

Demand for privacy. As curiosity becomes a habit, some will move the computer to a more private location, perhaps in a room

While Pavlov worked with dogs to demonstrate the principle of conditioning, another scientist worked with birds. B.F. Skinner was a psychologist who developed what came to be known as the "Skinner Box," a device in which he studied the behavior of pigeons. In a case of truth-is-stranger-than-fiction, much of Skinner's research was underwritten by the American government, which hoped Skinner could train homing pigeons to operate as kamikaze navigators aboard missiles.

with a lock on the door. They may rearrange the furniture so the computer screen is not visible by others in the room. Most often they will become easily irritated when interrupted while on the computer.

Disregarding other responsibilities. Some people can become so absorbed in their online activities that they no longer attend to household chores or other family activities. Time once spent cleaning the kitchen or doing yard work is exchanged for time spent surfing porn sites. Interest in hobbies and other recreational pursuits seems to diminish while time at the computer escalates. Time once invested in attending a child's school or sports activities dissipates, while online pursuits become the focus of considerable attention.

Change in sexual appetite. The sexual stimulation experienced in "virtual reality" causes changes in real-life sexual relationships. For some it manifests itself in an increased libido, or sex drive. For others, it's a change in regard to types of sexual activity desired. Still others withdraw and seem less interested in sexual contact. Having released sexual energy while online, little is left for "real" sex with their marriage partner.

from or struggled with pornography. For them, the story of Jesus' wilderness experience provides great hope. This is the story of how Jesus wrestled with Satan in the desert for forty days and emerged victorious from that wilderness experience.

In reading Mark's account of Jesus' baptism and temptation experience, note how quickly the author transitions from one scene to the next. In one sentence God declares his love for Jesus, and in the very next sentence the Spirit "sent" him into the wilderness to be tempted by Satan. In the Revised Standard Version, it translates that the Spirit "drove" Jesus out into the wilderness. In one moment Jesus celebrates his divine calling, while in the very next his mission is put to the test. In one moment a voice from heaven ordains his ministry, and in the very next he is sent into the wilderness to test his resolve to resist temptation and to fulfill his calling to his divine mission.

In the faith community we believe that God has called us to be his followers. We may not literally hear a voice speak from heaven, but we experience it nonetheless in our hearts. We sit in church on Sunday morning, celebrating our calling as Christians. But come Monday morning, we face temptations— temptations that may distract us from our true calling as Christ's disciples.

In the wilderness Jesus was tempted. The other gospel accounts of Jesus' wilderness experience speak of very real temptations like hunger. Jesus was tempted to turn stones into loaves of bread so that he could appease his hunger. There is nothing evil about hunger. Hunger is a natural consequence of being human. Our bodies exert energy, and that energy must be replenished by rest and nourishment. Similarly, there is nothing evil about sexual desire. Sexual desire is also a natural consequence of being human.

So how did Jesus resist the temptation to satisfy his need for hunger? And what would that mean for those who struggle with the temptation to satisfy sexual urges outside of the context of a marriage relationship?

The story of Jesus' wilderness experience shows us how Jesus kept his focus on God. Although faced with very real and powerful temptations, he chose to keep his focus on his baptism experience. He dealt with the temptation to satisfy his own needs by focusing on the reality that God had called him to serve a greater purpose. He dealt with temptation by staying focused on the belief that God would not abandon him.

Just because we Christians are called by God to follow and serve him, we are not exempt from a multiplicity of temptations. Jesus experienced this. But Jesus withstood the agony of temptation by never losing sight of his mission and ministry. For forty days Jesus experienced temptations, and for forty days he discovered the power that helped him keep his focus on the truth— that no matter what Satan would tempt him with, God would be with him. Like Jesus, we can rest assured that even in the wilderness experiences of our lives God will not abandon us.

Regardless of how stimulating or arousing or appealing the temptation may be, God is with us. Regardless of how destructive the dark forces of chaos might be, God does not leave us. Regardless of how much we fear our curiosity may have gotten out of control, God still believes in us.

And just as the text says, God provides angels to minister to us in our wilderness. If we dare to disclose our struggle to fellow believers, God will use them to minister to us. And just as God fortified and strengthened Jesus for his ordeal in the wilderness, so too will we be fortified and strengthened. When the forces of evil inundate us with sexual temptation to the point where we are at risk of being defeated, strength is available to us through God's network of messengers. We just need to muster up the courage to ask for their help.

The faith community recognizes and understands the reality that evil exists. There is evil in the world, and evil attempts to damage our relationship with God. We can be tempted and led astray if we are not watchful and careful. When it comes to pornography, Satan gains a foothold through our curiosity. Of course, curiosity in itself is normal. It is normal to wonder about the world and all that goes on within it. But curiosity can also be the first step to giving into temptation. Some may say, "I was just curious," but normal curiosity can start a process of escalation where they may want to explore "just a little more" or "just a little longer." Before they realize it, their curiosity has become a habit.

In the book of James (a New Testament letter that offers guidance regarding practical aspects of the Christian faith), it is written:

> *"Blessed is the man who perseveres under trial, because when he has stood the test, he will receive the crown of life that God has promised to those who love him. When tempted, no one should say, "God is tempting me." For God cannot bet tempted by evil, nor does he tempt anyone; but each one is tempted when, by his own evil desire, he is dragged away and enticed. Then, after desire has conceived, it gives birth to sin; and sin, when it is fullgrown, gives birth to death."*

JAMES 1:12–15, NIV

Evil is a very real presence in our world, and unless Christian men have a specific strategy to resist sexual temptation, they put themselves in jeopardy of being "lured and enticed" by their own desire. Yes, sexual desire is a God-given gift. However, people who use pornography to stimulate that desire risk developing unhealthy sexual desires.

Healthy sexual desire is found in the context of a loving, caring marital relationship. But pornography tempts people to find and explore that desire outside of the covenant relationship of marriage. When people see images of sexually attractive people engaged in intensely provocative activities, their sexual desire is activated or triggered and, if not controlled, can lead to fantasies which contribute to even more unhealthy sexual thoughts. Because their sexual fantasies are no longer focused on their marriage partner, their sexual desire is reduced to nothing more than lust.

It's essential that Christians challenge themselves to control their sexual desires. Failure to do so puts them at risk of embarking on a progression of sexual sin. The initial stage of the cycle is actually pleasurable. When humans first encounter pornography, there is an immediate biological reaction. Within milliseconds of viewing something sensual and provocative, the mind is flooded with sensory messages that convey the message that what is being looked at is good. Spiritually, however, Christians recognize the sinfulness of the material. But the images have a powerful, magnetic force, drawing them to look. Suddenly, the person is confronted with a battle; a battle between biological impulse and spiritual self-control. If in weakness persons use pornography, their spiritual resistance begins to erode, especially if the experience is reinforced by masturbation.

For Christians who are well aware of the sinfulness of pornography and yet choose nonetheless to use it, justification of the behavior is the next natural step. They have to rationalize his behavior in order to feel good about themselves, and this only reinforces the cycle. Typically, as the desire for sexual sin increases, the justifications for such behavior also get more elaborate. Justification is a very important factor in the sexual acting-out process. It minimizes the feelings of shame and guilt, which are meant to alert us that our attitudes, perceptions, and behaviors may be morally wrong.

With pornography so readily available on the Internet, Christians are faced with a very real threat to their souls. Like Dave, many Christians will be tempted. Some will resist the powerful grip of pornography, while others will become captive to it.

Strategies for Dealing with Temptation

Take Action Now

Sexual self-control is about more than abstaining from the use of pornography. It is about managing sexual desires and behaviors. Christians should develop an action plan to manage the powerful temptation of pornography. To help you resist the temptation toward cybersexual sin, we recommend you do the following:

Get rid of the computer. While this may not be an option for many people, others may have to ask themselves if they really need to have a computer in their home. In an age where computer terminals are available at most public libraries, you may need to consider living without one.

Change your Internet Service Provider. Many Internet Service Providers, such as America Online® and Comcast®, provide uncensored access to the Internet and World Wide Web. Although these are excellent service providers, the unmonitored access may be too problematic. You may want to consider Internet Service Providers that censor objectionable material.

Install protective software. Many software programs are available that screen and filter pornography. This is strongly recommended, especially for those who have children with access to the computer. Filtering products such as Net-Nanny® and Cybersitter® are good resources, but have limitations (primarily the need to know a porn sites address on the Internet), that prevent them from keeping up with the pace of new porn sites being added to the Internet each day allowing some porn content to get through to your screen.

Put the computer in a public place. It may not fit with your décor, but having your computer in the living room will discourage the temptation to use the computer to find pornography. It will be more difficult to be secretive this way.

Limit computer time. Covenant with yourself and with your wife to limit the amount of time you spend on the computer. Agree to not use the computer while alone, if possible. Some people find it helpful to set limits on their time. Instead of spending hours on the Internet, try spending one hour a day while other family members are around. If you can't follow this rule, maybe the computer has become a problem.

Delete previously saved material. Many men who have downloaded pornographic images are tempted to keep a collection of material. Keeping this material will only make it easier to relapse and repeat the very behavior you are trying to control. If material has been saved, permanently delete it.

Do something else. If you've found yourself spending time using the computer to access pornography, you need to find something else to do with that time. Whether it's stamp collecting or fly-tying, your thoughts and energy need to be focused elsewhere.

Ask yourself "Why?" Understanding the purpose behind using pornography may actually help you resist the temptation to use it. If you say that you use pornography because you feel lonely, then you may need to focus on developing friendships. If you think pornography helps reduce tension, then you may need to find other ways to manage your stress. If you say that you use porn because something's missing in your marriage, then maybe you need to attempt to resolve the problem rather than compound it.

Not convinced it's a problem? If you're not convinced that pornography is a problem for you and feel that it's mere recreational fun, then we suggest that you give it up for a while. Contract with yourself to refrain from using it for six months. If you aren't able to stay away from pornography for that brief period of time, then maybe you do have a problem after all.

Accountability

Secrecy is Satan's tool. The prince of darkness uses secrecy to undermine our resistance to temptation.

Most Christians use pornography in secret. While they would be too embarrassed to be seen at an adult bookstore, they choose the apparent anonymity of the Internet to access pornography. A driving force that perpetuates this behavior is secrecy. In not wanting their shameful behavior to be exposed, they will go to great lengths to erase the history and delete their computer's temporary Internet files. And all the while they work diligently to avoid being caught, Satan celebrates their gradual spiritual and relational decline. Secrecy gives Satan great satisfaction as Christians grow more and more distant in their relationships with their spouses and their relationships with their God.

A key to resisting temptation, therefore, is revealing the secret. Muster up the courage to admit it. Allow yourself to be held accountable by others, in addition to your spouse. Make connections with other Christians who similarly seek to protect themselves. Arrange for regular meetings or contacts with a peer group at your church, or connect with a trusted friend. Knowing that you have to tell someone else about your actions can provide powerful motivation to resist temptation.

Journaling

Another method for successfully resisting temptation is to monitor the factors that might put you at risk. Journaling of daily events is one way to help you develop hypotheses about circumstances that may weaken your resistance. We recommend that you keep a small, pocket-sized notebook with you at all times for approximately four weeks. This is not a "Dear Diary" type of journal but rather a place to record certain events that make you feel sexually tempted. Throughout the day take notice of when you may be dealing with sexual temptation. Note the time, the circumstances immediately before the event, your mood, a description of the event (e.g., content, duration, etc.), and your thoughts afterward. At the end of each day spend a few minutes reviewing your entries. Most likely, you'll notice a pattern. You may discover, for example, that the temptation is greater at certain times of the day. Or it may be influenced more by mood, or factors within your marriage, or circumstances at work. Realizing these patterns will help you learn what requires change.

Some use journaling as a therapeutic tool, writing their sexual autobiography. In fact, many of the vignettes included in this book are excerpts from the autobiographies of clients at The Hope and Healing Institute. They wrote their stories as part of the therapeutic process to learn more about themselves. In writing their stories, they became better able to reflect on their lives and, in so doing, became more aware of their strengths and coping skills. By writing your sexual history, you too can identify factors that put you at risk of succumbing to sexual temptation.

A WORD FROM DAVE

Fortunately, I have been able to get my behavior back under control. By the grace of God, I made a decision to tell my wife about my struggles. Together we spoke to our pastor, who put me in contact with a small group of men whose stories are similar to mine. Like messengers from heaven, these men have ministered to me in a way I never imagined. They have helped me to be honest with myself. They have helped me to be accountable. They have helped me become a more spiritually mature, more disciplined follower and servant of Jesus Christ.

3

Can You Handle the Truth?

On Confrontation and Confession

JAN AND STEVE'S STORY

I'm middle-aged, my boobs are beginning to sag, and I have hemorrhoids. To be sure, I wasn't feeling too good about myself. I used to be fairly confident about myself, but my self-esteem began to swirl down the drain when I discovered that my husband was using porn. How was I supposed to compete?

I've known my husband Steve for more than twenty-five years. We were high school sweethearts. We've raised four children, three of whom are now in college. Our youngest son is finishing his senior year in high school. It's always been our dream to make sure all our kids would go to college, and then we'd settle a bit and take some time for ourselves.

Our marriage had been good for the most part. Like most marriages, we've had our ups and down. But I'm not sure there is such a thing as a perfect marriage. We've had our share of financial struggles, but I think we've done well for ourselves. When the kids were younger I was a stay-at-home mom and Steve worked very hard to build his business. Once the kids hit high school, though, I found a job. We needed the money, and with the expense of college tuition for all three of our kids, we knew we'd have to tighten our budget. We weren't wealthy, but we were able to make ends meet. So, life was moving along in a good way. I was happy for the most part, beginning to dream of what life would be like for us as "empty-nesters."

My dreams, though, never involved the problems we were about to encounter. Never in my worst nightmare did I ever imagine that my husband had a problem with pornography.

It was about five years ago when we switched the computer's Internet service provider from a telephone modem to the high-speed cable. I was surprised that Steve was willing to pay the extra expense, but the kids were having to do so much online research for their homework assignments that it seemed reasonable. Not long after, though, we started getting emails advertising porn sites. I asked Steve about it and he told me it was not much to worry about; but I was worried. Worried about my kids. Frankly, I never gave much thought to worrying about Steve.

So, being a good, protective mom, I watched the computer history just to monitor what my kids were up to and one day I discover that the computer had been used to go to some porn sites. But the record indicated that it happened at a time when the girls were at a church retreat and our son was at a basketball game. I was hurt and angry. I didn't know how to confront him. I guess I was afraid I would find out that after all these years he found me less attractive than he used to. It took me a good week to muster up the courage to talk with Steve and when I did the conversation lasted no more than five minutes. He actually apologized for not telling me that he "accidentally" went into a Web site, not knowing that it was a porn site. He said he tried to click out of it as soon as he realized what it was. He assured me that he didn't tell me because he was concerned that I would be upset.

And I was upset. Not then. But over the next five years we have had this same conversation no less than half a dozen times. And each time he would become more and more angry with me, accusing me of being paranoid and overly suspicious. And each time I would confront him I would come away from the conversation wondering if I was the one with the problem.

But a few months ago I crawled off to bed early. It was a Friday night and I'd had an exhausting week. A few hours later I awoke to discover that Steve had not yet come to bed. I glanced at the clock. It was one o'clock. Steve usually is in bed by eleven. I figured he had fallen asleep on the couch. He's done that before and wakes up with back pain—and in a bad mood. So, to save myself the grief of living with a grump, I went downstairs to get him to come to bed.

I was shocked at what I discovered: Steve sitting at the computer looking at pornography. I gasped. He was startled and quickly turned off the computer monitor. No words were exchanged between us. I went back upstairs, took his pillows and tossed them on the floor outside our bedroom door. He could sleep on the floor for all I cared.

I didn't sleep a wink. I don't think I've ever been that upset.

The next morning I got up not certain what was going to be said or done. I made some coffee. I didn't know what else to do. When Steve came into the kitchen, I asked him if he wanted some coffee. It just seemed like the right thing to do. We sat at the kitchen table for the longest time in silence. I saw the pain in his face, and I'm sure he saw the pain in mine. I finally found the courage to speak. (Maybe God had given me the right words at this time, because I couldn't do all this by myself.) I told Steve I wanted to know everything. The truth. The whole story.

Steve told me that in these past five years he'd been battling with a desire to use pornography and losing. After all these years, after all the times I had confronted him, he finally confessed that what I had suspected was actually true. It was a surreal moment for me. Although blazing with anger that he had lied to me on those many occasions, I was relieved (for lack of a better word) to finally get the truth.

Steve told me that for him, porn was like a drug. Over time he wanted to do it more and more. The more he looked, the more he wanted. It started out of curiosity, he said, but within weeks he

No doubt about it, he had a choice. Nathan had no authority over him. David was the King. He knew he could dance around Nathan's accusation. He had the power and the authority and finesse to dodge the bullet of truth. But in that moment, David made a decision to become radically committed to moral purity. In that moment of truth, David was able to face his shame, the shame of realizing what he had done. Had he only taken a sheep from Uriah, David could have restored it a hundredfold. But he could not give back a life that he had destroyed. He could not give back a life he had taken away. He could not undo the past. There was no rewind button.

Sooner or later the truth about what we are doing is exposed. Maybe it will be when you get a call from Human Resources and they inform you that you have been fired for violating the company's Internet-use policy. Maybe it will be when your child stumbles upon something you downloaded but forgot to delete. Maybe it will be when you find yourself arranging for a real-life meeting with someone you have been cybering with. Maybe it will be when the knock at the door is not UPS delivery, but an agent from the FBI. Or maybe it will be when your partner asks, "Honey, how is it with you? Has it been a problem?" Maybe it will be when you read the story of David and when you get to Nathan's line, "You are the man," and you realize that God is talking to you.

What do you do when confronted with the truth? You have a choice. You can continue to live a life of deceit, deceiving yourself, deceiving your partner. Or you can do what David and Bathsheba did. You face the consequences. What happened to David and Bathsheba? Their first child died. It is inconceivable that God would cause the death of an infant because of his father's sin, and so it is not suggested that others who are guilty of sexual sin would be punished in such a way. But there will be consequences. And as it says in Scripture, the wages of sin is death.

When it comes to persons or couples struggling with cybersexual problems, something has to die. Old patterns of denial, patterns of self-deception, patterns of rationalization, all have to die. Are you afraid that maybe your marriage won't be able to survive if you disclose your struggle? There is no guarantee it will, but as Christians you have been given faith to trust in the power of resurrection. And before there is resurrection there must be death. For you, this might mean that certain aspects of that old relationship, old expectations, and old ways of relating have to die.

When faced with the truth, when faced with his shame, David accepted the consequences. And when he heard about the child's death, he got up, took a bath, covered his body with lotions, put on clean clothes, and went to pray in the house of the Lord. He came back again and ate, and then went in to comfort Bathsheba. Do not miss the powerful symbolism of what he did when he made a decision to be radically committed to moral purity. By accepting the truth about himself, there was no need to continue living a life of self-deception. He was washed clean. He was forgiven. He turned to a place of worship to give honor to God who made it possible. He nourished himself spiritually and physically and he pledged his love and support to Bathsheba.

Years later David wrote a psalm that has special meaning for those who have walked in the shadows of shame and self-deception:

> *The Lord is my shepherd,*
> *I shall not be in want.*
> *He makes me lie down in green pastures,*
> *He leads me besides quiet waters,*
> *He restores my soul.*
> *He guides me in the paths of righteousness*
> *For his names sake.*

Even though I walk
> *Through the valley of the shadow of death,*
I will fear no evil,
> *For you are with me;*
Your rod and your staff,
> *They comfort me.*
You prepare a table before me
> *In the presence of my enemies.*
You anoint my head with oil;
> *My cup overflows.*
Surely goodness and love will follow me
> *All the days of my life,*
And I will dwell in the house of the Lord Forever.

PSALM 23, NIV

As Christians we believe in the power of resurrection. We believe there is hope not only for the sinner, but also for those who have been sinned against. By the power of resurrection there is a second chance not only for those who go on living, but also for those whose lives have been destroyed by sin. We believe that the resurrection means that someday the tangled web we have created will be straightened out. Righteousness will be restored, and we will dwell in the house of the Lord forever.

Strategies for Confrontation and Confession

The purpose of any confrontation is to discern and determine the truth. The truth, however, can be difficult to face. Prayer, therefore, is an opportunity for you to seek guidance from God as you prepare to encounter the truth. Prayer will help you develop the appropriate tone for the conversation. Prayer will allow you to confront with supportive understanding and confess with resolute honesty. Prayer will help you prepare for what you may learn and discover in the process of confrontation. You are, after all, afraid of what you may find. You are concerned about your spouse's reaction. You may fear your own reaction. You may struggle with embarrassment over having to talk about sex and sexuality. Prayer will be an opportunity to contemplate these things and present them to God seeking guidance and wisdom.

For those who find it difficult to find words to express, the following prayers are suggested:

A Wife's Prayer

Gracious God, you know how nervous I am. I know something is bothering my husband, and there is part of me that is not wanting to face what it may be. But I think I know what it is, but I am just so afraid. Afraid of what I might discover about him; afraid of what this might mean about me. I'm just so afraid.

But I do trust you, O God, and so I pray for your blessing upon us in this difficult time. You blessed us on our wedding day when we made our covenant pledge to one another, promising to love each other for better, for worse, in sickness and in health. But this is not the kind of sick I anticipated, O God. I am sick in the heart and wounded in spirit. But you, O God, have blessed us throughout our marriage and I trust in your continued blessings as we try to work through this. You are our God and you brought us together and you have blessed us with a good history and I pray that our history will be a strong foundation to help us withstand this current storm.

I need your help, Lord. Help our marriage to be strong enough so that we can talk about this without anger and hostility. Help me to communicate my feelings to him while at the same time being understanding of his struggle. Help me to listen in a supportive way. Help me to choose my words carefully so that I am not judgmental, but encourage him to be the man you intend him to be.

The presence of your Spirit was apparent in the life of King David when he was confronted by the prophet Nathan. And so I pray, Lord, let your Spirit be upon us. May your Spirit grant us compassion, strength, and a resolution to make our marriage stronger than it was before. And give us both the strength to resist the temptations, which have drawn us away from each other and away from you. Amen.

A Husband's Prayer

Who have I been trying to fool, O Lord? You know my thoughts. You know what I have done. And you know my shame. I have been dishonest with myself and with my wife. And I certainly have failed to live the Christian life to which you have called me.

I do not understand why pornography has such power over me and why I find it difficult to resist the temptation to look. But I do know that you give strength to those who ask and through all my struggles I have been less than sincere in requesting your help. But now, O Lord, I need you to strengthen me. Not strength to resist, but the strength and courage to be honest with my wife. I am so afraid of how she will react. This is my problem, not hers, and I do not want to burden her or cause her pain. But it's as if I've been living a double-life, and in an awful way I feel I have betrayed her trust by keeping this a secret from her. Bless her, Lord. And by your Spirit, may I have the courage to be the man you intend me to be. Amen.

Setting the Stage

When people commit themselves to the process of confrontation and confession, much time and energy should be invested into preparation of what will be said. Obviously, this preparation is invaluable, as it will set the tone for healing to begin. Couples need to be cautious, however, in recognizing that "speaking" is only a fraction of the communication process. Of course you prepare yourself for what you want to say. But have you adequately prepared yourself to listen?

If you are praying for God's Spirit to guide you through a productive exchange of confrontation and confession, you may find inspiration in reading the story of Pentecost in the Book of Acts. When the Holy Spirit came upon those gathered in Jerusalem, a miracle happened:

> *Suddenly a sound like a violent wind came from heaven and filled the whole house where they were sitting. They saw what seemed to be tongues of fire that separated and came to rest on each of them. All of them were filled with the Holy Spirit and began to speak in other tongues as the Spirit enabled them."*
>
> *"Now there were staying in Jerusalem God-fearing Jews from every nation under heaven. When they heard this sound, a crowd came together in bewilderment, because each one heard them speaking in his own language.*
>
> ACTS 2:2–6

Of the countless blessings experienced that day, not the least of which was the gift of hearing. Though different languages were being spoken, the power of the Holy Spirit enabled them to hear and understand what was being said. And so, as you prayerfully prepare for confrontation and confession, you need to do more than anticipate your own words or tone. You need to focus attention on how well you will listen to each other.

Wives: Consider Tone, Timing, and Terrain

Pay attention to the manner in which the prophet Nathan approached King David. He was well aware of David's transgressions, but in confronting him, he elected to use a metaphor

In regard to paraphrasing, couples must understand that this skill is utilized throughout any conversation wherein clear communication is essential. It is not isolated to only the first few comments, but continues throughout the conversation even to the point of resolution.

Perception Check: A perception check is a communication skill in which you seek clarification on what you think you "see" happening. In a sense you are guessing what is going on, because you truly do not know. All you know is what you see and what you see may not be interpreted accurately. For example, in your conversation with your husband in which you are confronting his use of pornography, you observe him rubbing his forehead. Based on visual observation alone, you might conclude that he is angry with you. But your perception may not be accurate. You truly do not know exactly what he is feeling. And so you ask. In a non-judgmental manner you state your observation and offer an interpretation of what it might be, and then ask for clarification. For example, you can say, "I see you rubbing your forehead. I'm wondering if you are angry with me. Am I right?" Of course your intuition may be correct, but it also may be wrong. Your husband, instead, may be rubbing his forehead out of utter shame and embarrassment. If the conversation had continued with you believing that he was angry, the direction of the conversation may have taken a turn for the worse.

A key component to the perception check is the admission that you may or may not be accurate in your perception. You need to be able to communicate your perception without declaring the presumption that you have already reached the conclusion that it was accurate. The words you use are exceptionally important. The most effective perception checks begin with phrases such as: "I get the impression that…" "It seems to me that…" "I'm wondering if…" "It sounds to me as if…" "Is it possible that…" "I get the feeling that…"

After you state your observations, be sure to ask a question, so that your partner knows that you do not presume to be omniscient and you realize your perception may be inaccurate. Effective perception checks are followed with questions such as: "Am I right?" "Is that correct?" "Is this how you feel?" "Is that true for you?" Keep in mind there is no way for you to know with absolute certainty what the other person is thinking or feeling. You need to ask.

Time Out: When there is a conversation involving heightened emotion, one of the most beneficial interventions that couples can utilize is a "time out." This means that at any point in the conversation, either party has the right to request a time out at which point the conversation comes to an end. Especially when the conversation becomes unproductive, there needs to be a way to bring the conversation to temporary closure. But the key is "temporary." Whether the person requests five minutes, thirty minutes, several hours, or a day, the intention is to keep the conversation productive. It is not a way to getting-in the last word or cutting-off your partner who is saying something you do not want to hear. Neither is it a time to step away from the conversation in order to re-group and develop a new strategy in order to "win" the argument. If that is the intention, then a time-out would be nothing less than manipulation. Instead, the intention of a time out is to allow each person time to focus attention on resolving the issue at hand.

The person making the request for a "time out" must be specific about how much time is being requested. For example, "I need a time out. Let's take five minutes (or an hour or a day)." After that time is up, the person who made the request must return to the partner to reinitiate the conversation. A couple can take as many time outs as needed. If respectful of one another, couples can utilize this technique as a primary tool to transform potentially hostile arguments into productive, solution-focused conversations.

A WORD FROM STEVE

Dear Jan,

I don't know if you realize it, but today is an anniversary, of sorts. It was exactly a year ago that you discovered me at the computer. It was the worst day of my life. But in a strange way, it was also the best. I will never ever forget the disappointment on your face when you walked in on me. And I will also never forget your courage to force me to face up to what I was doing to myself (and to you). For too long I was too afraid to face up to the truth about myself. And you, my sweet bride, had the courage to confront my problem.

When I look back at the changes in our marriage in this past year, I can't help but feel glad for the changes we have made. Our communication is better (way better) and I feel as if I understand you and you understand me like never before.

Thank you, Jan. For everything.

Love, Steve

Can You Forgive Me?

On Forgiveness and Reconciliation

KATHY AND TOM'S STORY

I had long suspected that Tom was using the computer to look at pornography, but every time I confronted him he assured me that nothing was going on and that I was just being paranoid and distrusting. There was one occasion when I checked the computer history and discovered that he had gone to some pornographic Web site. When I asked him about it he told me that some guy from the office had sent him something as a joke. He acted as if he was deeply offended and morally outraged that his friend would do such a thing. He said he didn't want to tell me because he didn't want me to be upset.

That is what he said, but deep in my heart I knew it wasn't true. He lied to me.

I know this because I walked in on him and saw for myself exactly what he was doing. He was sitting there at the computer looking at an incredibly graphic picture. And he was masturbating.

It was bad enough to have walked in on him, but his reaction actually made me hurt even more. He suggested that I was over-reacting. He said things like, "It didn't mean anything" and "I didn't mean to hurt you" and "This wasn't about you, it was about me" and

"It doesn't mean I don't love you, or want you" and "It doesn't mean anything is wrong with 'us.'"

All I could do was stand there and cry.

He slept on the couch that night. And the next day we didn't talk about it. Actually, we didn't talk about it for days. Days of silence between us. I wanted to know what was going on with him, but I was afraid to ask. Maybe I was afraid of the answer.

After several frustrating days of not dealing with this issue, Tom finally broke the silence. He came home early from work and told me he had a confession to make. He told me he had a problem with looking at pornography on the computer. He said he wanted to stop, but it was like he couldn't help himself. He said he didn't mean for this to ever be a problem, but over time, he became more consumed with it.

He asked me to forgive him.

Of course I said yes. It is what I was supposed to do. He said he was sorry. I could see the regret and remorse on his face. There was sadness in his eyes. What else was I supposed to say but, yes, I'd forgive him.

But that didn't make the pain and confusion go away.

Over the next few months, I struggled with trying to understand Tom's desire for pornography. I wanted to be supportive of him, but I couldn't help but feel angry, sad, and resentful. I was angry at Tom and at our culture that seems so preoccupied with sex. I was sad that something might be wrong with our marriage; sad that he might not find me attractive anymore. And even though Tom finally admitted he had a problem, I still resented that he had lied to me all those times.

I tried to talk to Tom about how I felt, but it was as if my feelings fell on deaf ears. He would have a glazed-over look in his eyes, like he was looking at me but not listening. Over and over he would tell me that he was sorry but didn't know what else to say. And so after a while he said nothing at all, telling me that I had to get over it.

It made me wonder if he even cared. It was depressing. I cried myself to sleep many nights. I knew he heard me, but why didn't he do or say anything? Why not just touch me on the shoulder and let me know everything would all be ok? Just say or do something!

I just wish he would understand what this has been like for me. Doesn't he care that I lay awake at night worrying if our marriage will survive? Doesn't he notice that I have felt so sick over this that I am hardly eating? Does he realize that this is about me too?

Despite Tom's reassurances that he would not look at pornography again, the trust had been broken. I said I forgave him, but I wonder if I really ever did. My feelings were like a mixture of guilt and anger: guilt that I can't seem to forget what he had done; anger because it seems so unfair that I even have to deal with something that I'm not responsible for.

He asked me to forgive him and I said I did. But why can't I forget? Why can't I get over this?

Cybersex: A Breach of Fidelity

"I didn't mean to hurt you." "This wasn't about you, it was about me." "It doesn't mean I don't love you, or want you." "It doesn't mean anything is wrong with 'us.'"

These are typical reactions from husbands offering assurance to their wives that their cybersexual behavior has minimal effect on their marriage. These sorts of comments are not surprising, since most men who use cyberporn actually believe that their behavior has little to no negative effect on their lives or relationships. But these comments stem from a perception wherein they consider the use of pornography to be "recreational." Their wives' perception, however, is radically different. Wives consider the use of pornography to be a breach of trust in the marital relationship.

In the year 2000, there was an extensive research study of 9,265 people who admitted to using the computer to view pornography or engage in cybersex. Participants in this study responded to an online survey posted on the MSNBC website over a seven-week period. In this study, two questions examined how pursuing online sexual materials may have interfered with or jeopardized certain aspects of respondents'

- Poor communication between partners.
- Not spending enough time working to save the relationship.
- Intense, unresolved anger.

It's important for couples to think about and reflect on the obstacles that might hinder renewal and restoration of the relationship. Husbands and wives need to be honest and open with themselves and with each other. Sometimes, it can be very insightful to ask your spouse what they see as a potential obstacle for you. This is risky. Sometimes feelings can be hurt, and you can be shocked by what your spouse may say. But then again, who will know you any better than your spouse. The tendency is to feel a bit resistant when we are told about our faults. It's natural to feel some defensiveness. But if this form of sharing and communicating is done with a loving and caring attitude, the walls of resistance often begin to tumble down. Insights and revelations about oneself begin to evolve, and this knowledge can go a long ways toward healing the relationship.

"To forgive is to set a prisoner free—
and discover that the prisoner was you."

LEW SMEDES

Forgiveness
as a Reciprocal Process

Beverly Flanigan is another author who has written about forgiveness.[6] She developed what is known as the "Transactional Model of Forgiveness." This model is helpful in understanding how Christian couples can follow Christ's admonition in the eighteenth chapter of Matthew.

The key premise of Flanigan's transactional model is that every relationship has rules. Some rules are unspoken, but these rules are present and affect the relationship in some way. She suggests that early on in relationships people begin to establish rules, for example a rule regarding honesty and truthfulness. If you break something that belongs to your spouse or friend that is important to him, do you tell the truth or make up some excuse? In another example, if your spouse gets a new hairstyle that she really likes but you dislike, do you share your opinion or just agree with her? There are various "rules" in relationships and they are not exactly the same for all relationships.

Whether spoken or unspoken, every couple has developed some "rule" regarding the use of pornography and cybersex. If the rule establishes that this type of activity is not acceptable, then engaging in such activity is a violation of the rule in the marriage. Consequently, an injury to the relationship occurs, and trust has been broken.

Flanigan's forgiveness model emphasizes that forgiveness and reconciliation is a reciprocal process wherein both parties have an active role. To achieve genuine forgiveness and reconciliation, both parties must be involved. Both parties must recognize the violation. Both feel bad, but the injurer feels particularly guilty. All the while, though, both continue to believe that the "rule" between them was, and still is, good. One party made a mistake, that's all. However painful the mistake might be, both people want to adhere again to the original rule they developed together. The contrite member can apologize and make promises. In response, the violated person can condemn or even punish the offender. In the end, apologies are accepted. The anger passes, and both people voluntarily agree to commit themselves to their original rule about how they should treat each other. They may even decide to change the rule a little; but both people agree to abide by that rule.

The model diagramed in Table 4-A illustrates the transactional or reciprocal nature of forgiveness and reconciliation. In marriage relationships, both partners have an active role. The process begins with a confrontation. The offended spouse must have the courage to confront the partner (see chapter 3). The pornography-user must allow himself to be held accountable. At this stage in the process husband and wife must spend considerable time in conversation discussing the nature of the offense and identifying what "rules" in the relationship have been broken as a consequence. Failure to adequately identify the rule will derail the forgiveness/reconciliation process. The offended spouse must be able to verbalize and articulate the reasons why the behavior was wrong while the partner

TABLE 4-A

A Transactional Model of Forgiveness and Reconciliation[7]

OFFENDED SPOUSE	PORNOGRAPY-USER
Accuses the porno-user of violating a relationship rule	Apologizes for breaking the rule
Summarizes the reasons the behavior was wrong	Listens and accepts
Expresses rage, sorrow, and a desire to punish the porno-user	Accepts this punishment
Seeks assurance the offense will not be repeated	Promises to never repeat the offense
Accepts promises and demands no further "payment of debt"	Trusts that forgiveness is permanent
Recommitment to re-established or new rules	Recommitment to re-established or new rules

engages active listening skills. The partner must resist defensiveness and focus on understanding how the online sexual activity affected the other.

On a visual diagram, the process may appear mechanical and void of emotion. On the contrary, though, when forgiveness and reconciliation is a reciprocal process, it is imperative that the couple permits (and encourages) the healthy expression of emotion. As described earlier in this chapter, wives experience a wide range of emotions when they discover that their husbands are using Internet pornography. The husband must allow the wife to express these feelings. The pornography-user, though, also is experiencing emotions and those too must be expressed. Couples may need to seek professional guidance if both parties are experiencing deep resentment or rage. But where this transactional model is most effective is when the pornography-user comes to fully comprehend the nature of the offense and express true contrition, guilt, and sorrow for the behavior.

The goal of this transactional/reciprocal model is the reestablishment of trust. A relational rule has been broken and the couple must work collaboratively to either recommit to the rule or establish a new rule to put in its place. Reciprocally, wives and husbands must seek assurance and offer promises that the offense will not be repeated. Collaboratively, wives and husbands must covenant with each other that behavior in the future will be radically different, and trust that the forgiveness is permanent.

Action Steps in the Reciprocal Process

To forgive and to reconcile are verbs and as such are "action words" requiring people to engage their emotional and spiritual energy to heal and save the relationship. Each partner plays a critical role in making this happen. Let's take a look at important actions that will facilitate this process.

The Wife

1. Pray for your husband and yourself every day. Pray for renewed trust. Pray for honesty and openness

2. Be patient. Change takes time, especially if the problem is deep seated and serious. Sometimes relapse is a part of recovery. This is not an excuse to repeat the offense, but you have to be realistic. Some problems take time to fix. Try to be understanding, even though it may hurt to hear of a relapse. You need to communicate to your husband what form of a relapse is totally unacceptable. Working toward reconciliation is about facing reality, not denying it.

3. Expect your husband to change. He must clearly hear from you that you expect him to change. Be loving, but also firm.

4. Give yourself permission to have your feelings. You have a right to your feelings. They are yours. Feelings are normal. If you have been hurt, then you have a right to feel hurt. If you are angry, it's ok to be angry. Let your feelings out, and don't bottle them up inside. Don't be ashamed or embarrassed to have and express your feelings. Cry them out if you need to. Let your husband know exactly how you feel. It's very important he clearly understands the depth of the pain that has been caused. This can help prevent him from acting out again.

5. Give yourself permission to take your time to heal as well. Recovery is often focused on the husbands "problem" and wives are left out of the healing process. This leads to isolation and puts one at risk for depression. Find trusting people you can talk to about how you are doing as well.

6. Try to understand and recognize you might need to make some changes in the marriage as well. Listen to your husbands concerns. Talk about concerns with an attitude of openness. Work together and support each other in every step of this journey.

The Husband

1. Take responsibility for your actions and communicate clearly to your wife what it is that you are apologizing for. Avoid ifs, ands, or buts. The process of forgiveness and reconciliation will be derailed if you use language that shifts blame or responsibility onto your wife. The word "if" is particularly damaging. For example, saying "I'm sorry if this upset you" does very little to encourage forgiveness. You are implying that you do not know whether or not you did anything wrong. The word "but" also confounds the problem because it declares that anything you said before was meaningless. For example, if you say, "You know I love you and prefer to be with you and I know I shouldn't have looked at those pictures but I was horny and you didn't want to have sex." The word "but" is a clear signal to your wife that perhaps you are trying to affix blame on her and that you may not be as loving and loyal as you suggest.

2. Pray for your wife's healing as well as your own. Pray that you may be able to help her to trust you again. Recognize your wife is going through recovery just like you. Be patient with her. Ask her what she needs from you to be able to rebuild trust. Communicate directly and don't dance around the issues.

3. Remember those sayings like "The proof is in the pudding" or "Actions speak louder than words"? It works

this way in recovery, too. Forgiveness is more likely to occur when your wife sees you making real changes. This can be a change in the way you act or talk to her. The best way to build forgiveness is to put your wife's needs before your own. Demonstrate sincere repentance by explaining to her how you are going to change your attitudes and behaviors in the future. Give her specific examples, like "I will make sure I have deleted

Depression and Anxiety Take Their Toll

Depression and anxiety are the most common emotional states reported by women upon the discovery of marital infidelity, including the discovery that their husbands have breached the marriage covenant on the Internet. Whether viewing pornography or engaged in an "online affair," the reaction to the indiscretion and infidelity often leads to mood and anxiety disorders.

The National Institute of Mental Health has identified key symptoms that indicate the presence of depression and/or anxiety.[8]

Warning Signs of Depression

- Persistent sad, anxious, or "empty mood" feelings of hopelessness, pessimism
- Feelings of guilt, worthlessness, helplessness
- Loss of interest or pleasure in hobbies and activities that were once enjoyed, including sex
- Decreased energy, fatigue, being "slowed down"
- Difficulty concentrating, remembering, making decisions
- Insomnia early-morning awakening, or over sleeping

all pornography on the computer, every picture," or "I've changed my computer screen name so the people I have previously chatted with will no longer be able to contact me. I'm breaking off all relationships I developed while online." Remember, relationships and feelings are very fragile. No one likes to get his or her feelings hurt or have trust undermined. If you make a promise to change, then you must do your best to

- Appetite and/or weight loss or overeating and weight gain
- Thoughts of death, or suicide; suicide attempts
- Restlessness, irritability
- Persistent physical symptoms that do not respond to treatment, such as headaches. digestive disorders, and chronic pain

Warning Signs of Anxiety

- Persistent worrying. The worrying can be accompanied by physical symptoms such as fatigue, headaches, muscle tension, irritability, twitching, sweating, and hot flashes.
- Repeated and intense episodes of fear accompanied by physical symptoms such as chest pain, heart palpitations, shortness of breath, dizziness, or abdominal distress
- Overwhelming anxiety and excessive self-consciousness in everyday situations. A fear of being watched or judged by others in social situations. Fearful of being humiliated by one's own actions.

Third, pornography affects the individual. Research indicates that it is possible to develop an addiction to pornography. What may have started as mere recreational use becomes an obsession. Like a drug, the individual uses pornography more frequently than intended. The type of material viewed escalates from erotica to hardcore. In order to achieve the same level of sexual arousal as before, the individual requires pornographic images that are increasingly more intense and graphic. The individual begins to disregard responsibilities at home or work while his time and energy are absorbed in the use of pornography. The individual continues using pornography even though he recognizes that it is having a harmful effect on himself and his relationships.

Justification

Christians know that the use of pornography is inappropriate. They are well aware that the use of pornography is a sexual sin that dishonors God and distorts their relationship with God and can potentially distort their relationship with wife and family. But they continue to use it. The choice to use pornography is driven, though, by a negative thought process known as "justification." Justifications are excuses that echo inside a person's mind giving them an excuse to use pornography. The problem, however, is that in most cases the thought-process is faulty. In Tom's situation, he knew that porn was wrong, but he exercised very little self-control or restraint. He justified what he was doing by allowing irrational and incorrect thoughts to direct his use of porn.

Some of the more common justifications include:

- "It's not like I don't love my wife. It's just for fun."

- "I just need sex more than my wife does."

- "It's not as bad as guys who go to prostitutes."

- "It could be worse. I could be having a real affair."

- "If I was getting more sex at home, I wouldn't need to do this."

- "At least it's not kiddie porn."

- "It helps me relax."

- "I'm lonely and I get to talk with others who know what I'm going through."

- "I only look at pictures once a week; it's not like I have a real problem."

- "If I don't masturbate regularly, I feel like I'm going to explode."

Musterbating

No, it's not a typo. This is not about *masturbation*. This stinking-thinking process is about faulty expectations wherein a person's irrational beliefs put unreasonable demands on themselves and others. Albert Ellis calls this type of faulty thinking "musterbating."[4] People rationalize their use of pornography if they believe that their expectations are not being met. People who "musterbate" have thought processes which reflect a sense of what "must" or "should" be occurring in their sexual relationship. In a sense, they believe that there are certain rules in regard to sex. When the rules are not being followed, there is disappointment and frustration.

Couples need to discover what these rules are and determine whether there is common agreement or if the expectations are unreasonable. For example, a husband might believe that in a healthy marital relationship a man and a woman should make love three times per week. The wife, however, believes that in a healthy marital relationship the sexual contact should occur once per week. The issue, though, is not over who is right and who is wrong. They both have expectations and rules in regard to the frequency of sexual intimacy. However, if one or both of them maintains the position that their view is correct and the other's faulty, there is potential for conflict. If husband and wife are not able to communicate and come to an agreement, there will be unresolved conflict.

The use of pornography introduces and reinforces faulty expectations. By viewing pornographic material or participating in chatrooms or newsgroups, a person develops beliefs and attitudes regarding sex and sexuality. This information, though, is usually inaccurate and yet the individual develops a sense that what they are experiencing is normative. The individual develops beliefs about the "rules" of sex, and over time these beliefs become more solidified and inflexible. In pornography, for example, women are portrayed as being multi-orgasmic and insatiable in their sexual desire. As a man is repeatedly exposed to this depiction they develop a sense that his wife "should" have multiple orgasms and she "should" be interested in sex far more frequently. Similarly, a man who views pornography and experiences women crying out in orgasmic ecstasy develops a rule that this is the epitome of expressing sexual satisfaction. With such expectation, the husband will be disappointed if his wife's experience is more subdued.

Evaluating Tom's "Stinking Thinking"

Tom's story, at the beginning of this chapter, demonstrates how faulty assumptions about pornography and "stinking thinking" led to an escalation of sexually inappropriate behavior.

Tom's use of pornography was getting out of control. Over time, he began to desire more and more pornography. Looking at a few pictures no longer satisfied his desire and craving. In his mind, he needed more. It became difficult for him to stop himself and control this desire. He justified his actions, which led to lying to his wife about why he was going to the bedroom at night. Sometimes, he really planned on working on the computer. But more often than not, he used the work excuse to cover his tracks. He even started to tell his wife he needed to work on the computer several hours before he actually went to his bedroom. He was practicing deception and becoming more confident as he practiced it. He became "comfortable" in lying. Tom illustrates this process very well when he stated, "my confidence in hiding all this got better."

Tom's deception was very conscious. He began to lie, justify his lying, and tried to block out any guilt and shame. At first, this was hard to do. He felt very guilty. But like many men, Tom's use of pornography reached the point where it became obsessive. He found it very difficult to stop and get control of himself.

As Tom became "more comfortable" in surfing the Internet for pornography, he also took more chances. He began to look at pornography when his children were home, a boundary he previously was unwilling to violate. He convinced himself he would not get caught, and though he felt guilty knowing the children were upstairs in their rooms next to his room, he began to feel less guilty over time. He began to believe since he had never been caught, he had perfected his strategy quite well. He convinced himself the children would never walk in on him, and if they did, he strategically planned a response. He anticipated a problem, but rather than eliminate the behavior itself, he found ways to perpetuate his situation. He learned how to quickly cover up the pictures on the computer monitor so no one would know what he had been looking at, only magnifying the risk that his behavior would escalate.

Feeling less guilty over time is a common dynamic in the escalation of this process. It's another example how justification or rationalization can deaden the feelings of guilt during the quest of fulfilling sexual desire. Tom felt some guilt when looking at pornography, but he compartmentalized it, or simply made the guilt go away for a while so he could complete the act. He told himself they were just pictures. He had convinced himself that it was normal for women to act and dress like the women in the pictures, and when his wife did not meet this expectation, he became angry with her and felt rejected. He turned to the pictures for comfort and pleasure. He made one excuse after another.

This is a common sequence of events for many men. Guilt usually follows the use of pornography, and sometimes even deters someone from looking at it for a period of time. Once the desire returns however, and grows in strength and power, justification returns, and the cycle is repeated. Sometimes this cycle or pattern is repeated over and over again within a very short period of time. For others, the pattern is less frequent. Instead of looking at pornography once a day, it's looked at for a couple of hours during the week. Regardless of the pattern established, the frequency of use, risk-taking, an escalation will continue.

In Tom's case, his excitement for pornography waxed and waned. He began to escalate by going to pornography sites on a regular basis, identifying his favorite sites so he could go back over and over, collecting pictures, and then masturbating to them. When pornography was reinforced by the pleasure achieved thru masturbation and orgasm, his desire for this type of feeling and sensation became stronger. Even this wasn't quite enough for Tom, as he discovered chatrooms and started talking with others about fantasies he had about his wife and other people. Ultimately, he justified chatroom conversation as acceptable because he really didn't know anyone personally, and besides, other men chatted in explicit ways as well.

Tom knew his behavior was wrong. There were times his desire to stop was also very strong, and sometimes he would win this battle. There were times he clicked on the computer, was tempted to go to a pornography site, but did not go. He felt relieved and good about this decision. He prayed for self-control. When attending church, he felt ashamed and guilt-ridden, often feeling the pastor's sermons on sin were directly meant for him. But like many good men of faith, sometimes problems can get out of control. The intensity of the escalation process catches people off guard. What appears as one small, harmless justification leads to a web of lies and secrecy. This process caught Tom off guard. It was like he was ambushed from behind. The destructive lure and power of pornography hit him when his guard was down. He was held captive.

Tom fought hard to face these issues and is stronger today than when he first discovered Internet pornography. He freely admits it is a tough battle to fight. Sometimes he's relapsed and used pornography again. He felt bad about each relapse, but had the courage to recommit to change. He was able to identify his thought patterns and assumptions about pornography and how they reinforced and escalated. This awareness and courage will help him in the fight to win this battle at some point, once and for all.

Scriptural Guidance for Repentance

On day Peter and John were going up to the temple at the time of prayer—at three in the afternoon. Now a man crippled from birth was being carried to the temple gate called Beautiful, where he was put every day to beg from those going into the temple courts. When he saw Peter and John about to enter, he asked them for money. Peter looked straight at him, as did John. Then Peter said, "Look at us!" So the man gave them his attention, expecting to get something from them.

Then Peter said, "Silver or gold I do not have, but what I have I give you. In the name of Jesus Christ of Nazareth, walk." Taking him by the right hand, he helped him up, and instantly the man's feet and ankles became strong. He jumped to his feet and began to walk. Then he went with them into the temple courts, walking and jumping, and praising God. When all the people saw him walking and praising God, they recognized him as the same man who used to sit begging at the temple gate called Beautiful, and they were filled with wonder and amazement at what had happened to him.

While the beggar held on to Peter and John, all the people were astonished and came running to them in the place called Solomon's Colonnade. When Peter saw this, he said to them: "Men of Israel, why does this surprise you? Why do you stare at us as if by our own power or godliness we had made this man walk? The God of Abraham, Isaac, and Jacob, the God of our fathers, has glorified his servant Jesus. You handed him over to be killed, and you disowned him before Pilate, though he had decided to let him go. You disowned the Holy and Righteous One and asked that a murderer be released to you. You killed the author of life, but God raised him from the dead. We are witnesses of this. By faith in the name of Jesus, this man whom you see and know was made strong. It is Jesus' name and the faith that comes through him that has given this complete healing to him, as you can all see.

Now, brothers, I know that you acted in ignorance, as did your leaders. But this is how God fulfilled what he had foretold through all the prophets, saying that his Christ would suffer. Repent, then, and turn to God, so that your sins may be wiped out, that times of refreshing may come from the Lord.

ACTS 3:1–19, NIV

The Book of Acts is perhaps one of the more neglected books of the New Testament. Most are familiar with the Gospels of Matthew, Mark, Luke, and John. We read the Gospels that tell of the events of Jesus' birth, ministry, death, and resurrection. And many of us stop reading the Bible at the conclusion of each of these four gospels, thinking in a way that is where the story ends, with Jesus' resurrection. But there is more to the story.

While the Gospels end with the stories of Jesus' resurrection, the Book of Acts begins and ends with stories of the ongoing miracle of the resurrection of others. To be sure, we do not have people raised from graves as was Jesus, but we have people raised from certain kinds of graves, nevertheless.

Just as the Gospels conclude with the message that crucifixion and death are not the final words, the Book of Acts proclaims that the power of resurrection, by the grace of the Holy Spirit, is still possible. Lameness, deafness, blindness, disease, and physical and mental disabilities are not the final words about life. Healing, health, strength, sight, and vitality are the final words. After his own victorious resurrection, Jesus offers the power of resurrection through his life-giving Spirit. It is God's intention to continue the process of resurrection so that in place of discouragement and defeat, people can turn their lives around and experience renewal. By the grace of Jesus Christ, you can experience new life.

But how? How might you experience the power of resurrection?

Insight is found in Peter's sermon to the crowd at Solomon's Portico in the Temple where he says, "Repent then, and turn to God so that your sins may be wiped out, that times of refreshing may come from the Lord."

And what does it mean to repent? It means to change. The key to resurrection and new life is change.

When the author of the Book of Acts described this event in Jerusalem he used one of the classic Greek words for repentance:

to use pornography. To begin this process, couples are encouraged to ask themselves the following questions:

1. How frequently would you want to engage in sexual intimacy with your partner?

2. What are your expectations regarding initiation of sexual intimacy? Who should do what and when?

3. Consider five things about yourself that you might change (in regard to sexual intimacy) with your partner. Identify those statements that include the words "must" or "should."

4. Consider five things about your partner that you might change (in regard to sexual intimacy). Identify those statements that include the words "must" or "should."

5. How has the use of pornography benefited or helped you?

6. How has the use of pornography benefited your partner?

7. Has pornography helped you to better understand the needs/desires of the opposite sex? What have you learned?

8. If you have used Internet pornography, identify the excuses/explanations you have used to justify the behavior.

9. Have there been any fantasies that have emerged since you began using Internet pornography?

10. If you could choreograph a "perfect" sexual experience with your partner, what would be involved? Who would do what? Are any of your ideas associated with what you may have viewed in pornography?

DROP
the erroneous or
dysfunctional thoughts.

For each of the responses to the ten items in step one, you and your partner need to collaboratively decide the degree to which the thought, belief, or expectation is healthy or reasonable. For each item, identify those thoughts/attitudes/expectations that may have been shaped by an experience with pornography. Recognize those items that may be reflections of minimization, justification, or "musterbations."

It is very difficult for most people to effectively evaluate whether their thoughts, beliefs, or expectations are dysfunctional and that is why it is so important to continue this exercise with your spouse or professional counselor. The intention, of course, is to sort out healthy thoughts from those that may cause damage to the relationship. It is imperative that couples approach this step by engaging the basic listening skills described in chapter three. It would be suggested that this step be entered into prayerfully. Challenge yourself to avoid defensiveness.

ROLL
these thoughts into something
more healthy and productive.

You need to identify an alternative interpretation. For example, if a husband's use of pornography has led him to the belief that most women "want" sex more than his wife does, his thought process is distorted by the thought that "my wife never wants to have sex." A healthier, alternative thought would be "My wife seems to be more interested in sex when..."

The challenge, therefore, is to transform dysfunctional cognitions into healthier, alternative thoughts that honor both the relationship and God.

Covenant Reminder

In the book of Genesis, there is the description of God's covenant relationship with Abraham. In setting himself and his descendents apart from others whose religions and beliefs were centered on sexual excesses and the worship of fertility gods, Abraham agreed to a procedure in which the foreskin of the penis is removed. It is the mark of the covenant, a powerful symbol of being in relationship with God.

Although circumcision is not a requirement for membership within the Christian community, it continues to be an option that many parents elect for their infant sons. The issue is one of hygiene and aesthetics. Nonetheless, for Christian men who have been circumcised: be reminded of your covenant relationship with God. Whether standing at a urinal, making love to your wife, or being tempted to masturbate, be reminded that your behavior is to be reflective of that covenant relationship.

6

Lost in the Wilderness
The Dangerous Terrain of Internet Chatrooms

MARY'S STORY

I am the mother of three wonderful children, and a wife to a husband who works very hard to provide for our family. This is my second marriage. My first marriage lasted about five years. We married young, were both immature, and we found our lives going in different directions. He wanted the fast life filled with material things and fun, and I wanted to settle down and have children. We quickly grew apart and divorced. My family found it difficult to accept the divorce, but that is partially my fault. I had given them the clear impression that things were fine. I was too embarrassed to openly admit my marriage was falling apart.

A few years later I met Donald. He seemed like Mr. Right; an answer to prayer. My family loved and adored him and saw that I was beginning to feel happy again. We started our family, went from an apartment to a house, and life seemed to be going along quite well. We both agreed I would be a stay-at-home mother. There were some financial sacrifices, but it was worth it. I felt I could give my children everything they needed, and I loved being a mother.

will reveal the way home. Yet each hilltop provides the same view as the one before. You begin to think that you are so lost that you will never find your way out again. You feel totally alone and vulnerable and frightened.

The Hebrew people knew the wilderness experience. After Moses led them in Exodus out of bondage in Egypt they wandered in wilderness for forty years. So when Old Testament authors speak of the wilderness, they evoke the memory of a time of lonesome wandering in a barren land; a time when the Hebrew people felt alone and forsaken by God.

A wilderness can be a physical reality, such as the wilderness in which the Hebrews wandered for forty years or Jesus' wilderness experience after his baptism. But the wilderness is more than a physical place. In the Bible, the wilderness is also a metaphor for times when we feel lost and lonely. The wilderness is a metaphor for times we find ourselves in danger or trouble. It is a symbol of times when we feel distant from God. The wilderness is a metaphor for the paths we take in our life's journey when we venture into dangerous terrain and discover how lost we have become. At times like that, we cry out to God, praying to Creator, Redeemer, Sustainer to rescue us.

These passages from the Book of Isaiah speak of a time when the Hebrew people were feeling lost. It was during the time of the Babylonian exile. In 587 B.C., the Babylonians had invaded the city of Jerusalem and destroyed the Temple of Solomon. Many of the Hebrew people were forced into exile, living in the barren, arid land of Babylon. It was as if they were again wandering in the wilderness.

In chapter thirty-five, the prophet Isaiah describes what would happen if God would appear in the wilderness. The dry and barren land will burst forth in bloom; then waters will rush out to fill streams and pools, and green grasses will grow. The wilderness will be transformed. And in the midst of its vast desolation a road will be built; a highway so broad and wide that shows the people of God the way back home to Jerusalem. And this highway will be visible from everywhere and so easy to travel on that no one would again get lost in the wilderness.

That highway will save the people of God from forever wandering hopelessly in the wilderness. They will travel on God's highway and they will know who they are and where they are to go. And they will know this is God's highway, according to the prophet Isaiah in chapter thirty-five because those who are blind will be able to see, those who are deaf will be able to hear, those who are lame will leap like deer, and those who could not speak will sing for joy.

Jesus Christ is God's highway, God's presence in the wilderness.

Those whose lives have been affected by pornography and cybersex find themselves in wilderness. At the beginning of this chapter you read about Mary who found herself going down a dangerous path as she explored the world of cyber-sexual chatrooms. Others like her find themselves lost in the wilderness terrain of cybersex and Internet pornography. Like spending time in a real wilderness, their wilderness can leave them feeling lonely and hopelessly lost. By their own actions they have distanced themselves from marriage partners, family, and God. When they realize the mistakes they've made; when they realize how lost they have become, they look for a way out, a path, something that will show them where to go and how to get out of the wilderness.

The way out is found in Jesus Christ.

Strategies for Finding Your Way out of the Wilderness

Experts in the field of remote wilderness exploration will tell you that if you ever get lost, the key to survival is to stay calm. Those who panic tend to take action before thinking, and their chances for survival can be jeopardized. When lost, it is essential to relax and focus attention. Your chances for survival increase exponentially if you follow three primary survival strategies: First, get your bearings. Second, move in a constant direction (preferably using a compass). And, third, constantly scan the horizon for signs of potential rescue.

The Prayer of the Prodigal

When experiencing significant shame, many Christians find it difficult to pray, not knowing what words to use. After all, how does one approach God in the aftermath of sexual sin?

Like the prodigal son, the first step is to go home to be greeted by a forgiving father. It will be a humbling experience and your hesitancy may be in the scarcity of words and language to describe your emotions. It is suggested, therefore, that in your prayers you do the following:

Center your thoughts on the majesty of God. This is the great Creator, the maker of the heavens and the earth. This is your creator who formed you in your mother's womb. Center your thoughts also on God's son, Jesus Christ. By his birth, death, and resurrection, your sins have been forgiven. By his sacrifice you have the privilege to return to relationship with God. Center your thoughts as well on the Holy Spirit who has guided you to discover the error of your ways, inviting you to return to God. By centering your thoughts on God the Creator, Redeemer, and Sustainer, you will find the language to appropriately praise and celebrate your Lord. And in so doing, you will sense God embracing you, just as the prodigal's father greeted his wayward child.

Get Your Bearings

Having wandered into the dangerous terrain of Internet chat-rooms, Mary soon discovered the trouble she was getting herself into. Finding the way out of the mess she had created first required her to assess her situation. She knew she had made a mistake, that's for sure.

Make your confession. God already knows what you have done, so this is not an exercise in informing God of your actions. This is an opportunity for you to conduct a full inventory of your sin. Focus on the effect your behavior has had on your relationship with God, with others, and its effect on you. Consider the manner in which you should have conducted yourself and recognize how far from that standard you were.

Celebrate forgiveness. Whether tears of gratitude or joyful smile, allow God's Spirit to wash you clean of your sin. Unlike times before, however, when you offered glib and cursory confession, your current action is a pledge, a commitment to a different way of life. No longer will you offer prayers only in times of crisis or fleeting moments of remorse. Now you will celebrate your renewed relationship with God through a spiritual discipline of daily prayer.

Ask for divine guidance. Again, this is a time for you to consider what you need in order to stay committed to this renewed relationship with God, marriage partner, and family. Consider those factors that put you at risk of relapse. Give thought to circumstances that may compromise your sexual or moral sobriety. Do not leave it to God to magically protect you. In prayer, allow God's Spirit to help you devise and plan specific strategies to guard and protect you.

The primary means by which she was able to stay calm was prayer.

Her story is a marvelous example of an individual who upon recognizing her dilemma, turned immediately to God in prayer. It gave her focus. It allowed her to center and concentrate her focus on her redeemer. It allowed her an opportunity to make an accurate assessment of who she is and what she had done.

Mary prayed to strengthen her relationship with God and husband. Prayer and spiritual devotion helped her resist any future temptations to reconnect with the Internet and search out relationships on those days she felt down and discouraged. Through prayer she came to realize that the Internet was no longer an option for coping with loneliness. Sometimes people are tempted in their area of weakness or vulnerability. It's best to recognize that temptation to relapse will likely occur, but knowing this in itself provides strength to resist the temptation because one will less likely be caught off guard.

Move in a Constant Direction

If lost in the woods or wilderness, rescue can be dependent on whether you are walking in circles or proceeding in one constant direction. Whether it is north, south, east, or west, chose one direction and stay in that direction. Whether following the sun that rises in the east and sets in the west, or if your direction is guided by moss growing on the north side of trees, or whether you look toward the heavens to be guided by the North Star, your survival may depend on traveling in one set direction. And, of course, if you have a compass, use it!

When lost in the wilderness of cybersex and Internet pornography, set your spiritual direction to move constantly toward God. Avoid paths that may divert or distract you from returning to that relationship. Scripture serves as a compass to keep you on that path. It is suggested you design a schedule of regular Bible reading, doing so especially when in times past you strayed into using the computer for selfish reasons. At times of greatest weakness, God's Word will help keep you in the path toward redemption.

Continually Scan the Horizon

Persons who are trying to find their way when lost in the wilderness intuitively know to watch the horizon for signs of civilization. Especially in the dark of night, lights in the distance are a heartening discovery because it indicates that shelter and aid will soon be available.

Scanning the horizon means looking for community. It means actively searching for resources to assist you.

In relationships and marriages where one or both struggle with some aspect of the relationship, its acceptable and often wise to seek out counsel from other Christians. This can include seeking pastoral guidance, or professional counseling. Sometimes people are embarrassed to go to counseling, but don't let pride get in the way. Counselors are trained to help people who are stuck. They can shed light on the problems and offer solutions. Most clinicians are sensitive and realize clients are embarrassed to discuss their problems in such a setting, and you can be certain that an effort will be made to help you feel more comfortable.

Mary needed to repair the trust and bond with her husband. She needed to communicate her loneliness and needs for affection that were going unmet. She and her husband needed to talk openly about their marriage. Sometimes when couples struggle with this type of communication, or anger and tension is so strong that it feels unsafe to express oneself openly, a counselor can help couples break this impasse.

One night, Gary introduced to me to a game he called "truth or dare." He started the game by asking me to do silly things like jump up and down or make animal sounds. It was funny and we laughed a lot. We played this game every time he babysat me. One night, the game changed. We started out acting silly just like before, but as the game went on Gary dared me to touch his private parts. He told me touching his private parts was all part of the game and it would be a lot of fun. He took his penis out from under his shorts and told me to rub it for him. He told me to move my hand up and down, and he even showed me how to do it by putting his hand on top of mine. I did what he wanted me to because I was confused and too afraid to tell him no. He said I did a good job and I was winning the game. After a few minutes, Gary said the game was over. He removed my hand and put his penis back in his shorts.

Gary told me I should never tell anyone about this game because our parents would get mad and I'd get in trouble. This seemed con-fusing to me because I thought it was just a game, but since I didn't want to get in trouble or make Gary mad at me, I didn't tell anyone about the game. It was our little secret.

Over time, Gary's truth and dare game evolved and included much more touching than the first time we played. I touched his penis and he touched mine. It felt good when he touched mine. It sort of tickled. He told me the tickling feeling was good. He'd always tell me afterwards that the game was our secret and I'd get in trouble if I told. He also told me he'd be really mad at me if I told our secret and wouldn't play with me anymore. He said his parents would be so mad, I wouldn't be allowed to go swimming in their swimming pool, and so I kept my promise. The secret was safe with me.

As Gary's game evolved over the course of a year, my feelings about the game changed. It wasn't fun anymore. I felt like something was wrong, but I wasn't sure what to do about it and I didn't want to get in trouble. It seemed all Gary wanted to do when he babysat me was play that stupid game. Gary was sexually abusing me, but I didn't know that then. It was rather traumatic to me; I'll skip the grizzly details. It's still unpleasant to talk about it to this day. I never told my parents of the abuse until I got in trouble with the law. I'll talk more about that later.

■ ■ ■

The secret I kept about my abuse burned inside of me for a very long time, but like many victims of abuse I was too ashamed and embarrassed to talk openly about it. I was also a little afraid of Gary. He told me never to tell of our game, and since he was older than me, I listened. I also thought that if I kept it secret, then the bad feelings I had about the abuse and myself would somehow go away over time.

Gary and his family eventually moved away, so the abuse stopped. I missed Gary, but I was glad we didn't have to play the game anymore. I tried to forget about it, but I couldn't get it out of my head. I wanted to tell someone, but I was still afraid Gary would find out and we would get in trouble just like he warned.

To this day, I'm still not totally sure why I didn't tell my parents when I suspected something was wrong. I think they would've believed me, but something inside kept me from telling the secret. Maybe I really believed my parents would be mad and blame me for what happened. I also didn't want to lose Gary's friendship or not be able to swim in his pool. For a long time I believed I'd done something wrong and shouldn't have let Gary touch me. I felt I was to blame for not making him stop.

During my teenage years, I struggled with many issues that I now believe are directly connected to my abuse. I was often depressed, but put on this mask and tried to act like everything was OK. I had some friends, but it was hard to let anyone get close to me. I was afraid they would somehow find out about the abuse and stop liking me.

I tried hard not to think about it, but this became more difficult when I reached puberty. I liked girls, but there was a part of me that secretly worried I might be gay. I didn't have sexual feelings for guys so I told myself I mustn't be. But in the back of my mind, I always worried about it. I worried that if my peers found out I had been abused by a guy, they would think I was gay. I wanted to be invisible. I've learned this is a common worry for boys who've been abused by males. I felt so alone. I wondered what was wrong with me, but there was no way I was going to openly talk about this with anyone. I worried if I opened up just a little, someone would be able to figure out I'd been abused.

As I became more depressed, I felt like staying home more than going out with friends. I didn't go to football or basketball games like other kids my age. Home felt much safer than the social world of school. I was tired a lot, sometimes sad without knowing why, and my social confidence was in the pits. I knew I was missing out on life, but I really didn't care. The more socially isolated I became, the more depressed I felt. It was a very vicious cycle that I didn't know how to break.

The only friends I had at the time were two cousins, who introduced me to video games. I quickly became hooked on them because I could play by myself and safely retreat from the real world. Before long, I told my parents I needed a computer for school. I think they agreed because they hoped it would make me happy.

I quickly learned the ins and outs of computers, including the Internet. One day while working on a homework assignment, I went to a Web site I thought would be appropriate for the topic I was researching. To my amazement, pictures of hot-looking naked women popped up! I was excited by what I saw. I followed the link for a free tour of the site. Wow, more pictures!

I became addicted to pornography overnight. I never spent any money on buying porno pictures and I didn't need to—they were all free. I became so obsessed over time that I would keep my computer running all day downloading as many pictures as I could. I collected thousands of images every day, far too many to ever look at. So I'd save them onto discs.

Most nights I'd look at the pictures and masturbate. It made me feel good, at least temporarily. Sometimes I'd sit at the computer for hours, getting aroused, but holding off my orgasm until I found just the right picture that pushed me over the excitement edge. It was like I was in a trance, losing all perspective of time.

I kept my door locked so my parents wouldn't walk in on me. Sometimes they'd ask what I was doing all night in my room with the door locked. I'd just lie. I said I was doing a school project and needed privacy. They had no clue what I was really up to. If by chance they would walk in on me, I knew how to change the computer screen really fast and hide the pornography. I'd sometimes get mad at them and even yell at them if they interrupted me. It was like they were spoiling my private time.

I continued to go to school but didn't have many friends. My grades really suffered, and I lost interest in school altogether. Most of the time I daydreamed about the pornography I'd be viewing when I got home.

I thought about my sexual abuse often, but still kept it secret. My self-esteem was so low. I felt trapped. There were times I thought about suicide. I thought about hanging myself or shooting myself. The depth of my pain was too much to bear most of the time. Even though masturbation and pornography gave me some temporary relief, the problems were always there. It's like the more depressed and isolated I became, the more I escaped to my computer. I could control the computer. I couldn't control people.

One day while online, my cousin instant-messaged me. He suggested I contact this girl he'd met online. (I'll refer to her as Shayla, even though that's not her real name.) I sent her an instant message, and she responded right away. It was so cool. We chatted for a little bit, nothing too serious. Over the next few weeks, we struck up a friendship and shared more about ourselves.

Shayla lived with her parents, who argued and fought a lot, and she was very unhappy and depressed, just like me. I also found out that she was younger than me, a minor, in fact. But I didn't dwell on that too much. A girl was talking to me, taking interest in me even! Who cared how old she was?

She even shared with me that she'd been abused. I felt reassured that there was someone out there like me, someone who could relate to me.

I finally got up the courage and told her I'd been sexually abused when I was younger, and she was very understanding. She didn't make fun of me or reject me. She just had a way about her that made me feel truly understood.

I noticed my feelings for Shayla starting to grow. I had another reason for looking forward to coming home from school now. I hoped she'd be online so we could chat, but I never told her about my pornography problem. I didn't want to risk scaring her away. It's funny how I could tell her about my abuse, but not about my pornography problem. Maybe I didn't even realize how serious my problem was at the time I met her. But collecting porn pictures had become as much a part of my daily life as brushing my teeth. I didn't want to reveal that part of myself. I guess I was still keeping secrets.

One day Shayla suggested we send each other pictures of ourselves. I was excited about seeing what she looked like, yet nervous that she would think I was ugly and reject me. Plus, I knew in the back of my mind she was a minor. I was so needy for a friend; I didn't want her age to matter.

We each had digital cameras, so we took pictures and sent them to each other. She was so cute, I couldn't believe it. The next day, however, she wasn't online. My worst fear was confirmed: she thought I was ugly and didn't want to chat anymore. I was instantly depressed again, and felt sick to my stomach. I told my parents I had the flu and stayed home from school the next day.

I did nothing but lie around, feeling depressed. Later in the day, when I knew she was home from school, I got on the computer to see if she was online. She was. I wanted to send her an instant message, but I was afraid she would ignore me. I sat there, just staring at the computer screen. And then, she sent me a message. A friendly message. She apologized for not being online the previous day. We started to chat again. I was euphoric. She still liked me.

As time when on, I suggested we send naked pictures of ourselves to each other. To my delightful surprise, Shayla agreed. That was such a rush. I started to think of her as my girlfriend. Even though I didn't really know her, I thought I did, and her sending pictures to me made me feel she really cared for me. Sometimes, I masturbated to her naked pictures. I never told her that. But doing so made me feel closer to her.

One day, she suggested we talk on the phone and even meet each other. She lived in another state, so meeting didn't seem that practical, but I called her. Her voice was so cute. I was falling in love. Finally, a girl who liked me! I didn't care that she was a lot younger. She made me feel good about myself. That's all that mattered.

We arranged to meet. I was going to skip school, borrow my parents' car, and drive the three hours to meet her. I couldn't sleep the entire week. Thoughts of Shayla and the sex we might have consumed me.

As I was driving to meet her, though, I was tempted to turn around and go home. A voice in my head kept telling me this was wrong and I could get in trouble. But it was too late. I had to meet her and see who the girl of my dreams was, in person.

We'd planned to meet in a hotel room in a not-so-good part of town. I got lost a few times, but finally found the hotel. After parking the car, I took a deep breath and knocked on the door. The door opened, and to my surprise, I was tackled by three police officers who forced my hands behind my back and handcuffed them. They put me in a police car and drove me to jail. I was shaking all over and felt like I wanted to cry. It was the worst moment of my life.

I never did meet Shayla. I later learned she was scared of meeting me and told one of her girlfriends about our plans. Her girlfriend told her parents, who then called the police.

I was allowed to make one phone call from jail. That was the hardest phone call I ever made to my parents. I stuttered at first, but finally told my mother what happened. She cried a lot. I then told my dad. He was quiet. That meant he was too angry to say anything. I'd let both my parents down. I just wanted them to tell me everything would be OK. I felt so utterly alone.

The police were not supportive. In fact, I could tell they thought I was a bad person by the way they treated me and talked to me.

They thought I meant to harm Shayla, which was so not true. But they didn't believe me and made me feel like such a loser.

They fingerprinted me and took my picture. They told me I was being arrested. They advised me to call an attorney. Who would I call? I didn't know any attorneys. I had never gotten in trouble before. I didn't know what to do. I waited for my parents to come see me. That was longest wait of my life. I was put in a holding cell with some scary-looking men. They looked like hardened criminals.

After my parents posted bail, I was let out of jail and allowed to go home with them. The ride home was silent. I didn't really know what to say. I was ashamed and embarrassed. I just wanted to close my eyes and make it all go away. It didn't go away, though; it was just the beginning of a long and frightening ordeal.

My parents found an attorney for me. He explained how much trouble I could be in. I didn't really understand all the legal words he used, so I kept quiet. My parents did the talking for me. The first recommendation he made was to call up a counselor he had worked with and trusted. My parents called the counselor and set up the first session for me. I was so scared to go to counseling. As it turned out, this is the best advice I was ever given. It took time to trust my counselor, but when I did, I told him my life story.

What I learned from counseling was that the actions that got me into trouble with the law stemmed from my past sexual abuse. That doesn't excuse my behavior, but it helped me to understand why I did what I did. For years I'd tried to cover up the abuse and mask my feelings, but I paid a high price. It doesn't really seem fair I had to suffer so much. I lost perspective on reality. I used the computer to hide behind and create what I thought was a safe haven in the privacy of my bedroom. I've learned my emotional pain made me feel vulnerable, so I turned to the computer and pornography to escape reality. I created a fantasy world.

I saw and experienced the dark side of online pornography first hand. The use of pornography made me more depressed. It allowed me to maintain my denial about my own abuse. Then, when Shayla began showing an interest in me, I fantasized that she was my girl-friend—and we'd never even met before! But she filled the need I had for companionship. After I lost her, I was sad for a very long time.

I haven't talked with her since that fateful day of my arrest. I got rid of all my Internet pornography. Every last picture. I never want to go back to that darkness again.

Since then, I finished high school and completed college. I joined a young-adults Bible study. I still get depressed now and then, but I don't think about suicide anymore. I know it will take time to completely get over my depression. And, I haven't looked at any por-nography in a long time. I'm on my way to recovery. And, oh yes, I even found a girlfriend who's my age.

Now I tell anyone who's been a victim of childhood abuse that it's important to talk about it and understand how it can affect you. I also tell anyone who'll listen to stay away from online pornography. It nearly ruined my life. Thank God, I'm free.

The Impact of Child Sexual Abuse

The destructive cycle of child abuse is a real issue for many. Sex-ual abuse happens to both boys and girls of all ages. Some vic-tims of child abuse tell a trusted adult right away. This is a good thing. It stops the abuse from continuing in most cases. It takes a lot of courage for a child to disclose the abuse. However, many children are so confused, frightened, and ashamed, they keep their abuse secret for years, sometimes a whole lifetime, while suffering in silence. Some offenders scare children into keeping the abuse a secret. They tell children they will go to jail if caught. Some tell the child no adult will believe them and they will get into a lot of trouble. Offenders often tell children their mother will be angry and the abuse will lead to divorce. Some offend-ers are very clever in making the child feel they actively desired the abuse, and the child feels so guilty, they hide the secret, even from trusted adults or peers. Whatever the reason, children often are conflicted about reporting the abuse. They know or have a sense the abuse is wrong, but it's just too hard to tell.

Sexual abuse damages children's self-esteem and self-worth. They feel dirty, bad about themselves, and betrayed by a trusted adult. Sometimes children are abused by older children in their neighborhoods, a relative, or someone the family trusts, like a babysitter. Sometimes a victim has felt emotionally close to their offender, like a father figure. They are torn between reporting the abuse and possibly breaking up their family, and hurting the paternal figure's feelings. They take a protective role and actually take care of the offender's emotional needs. Regardless of the type of abuse or the relationship between victim and offender, the abuse can have long-term emotional effects. This can include struggling with trust and intimacy in adult relationships, even marriages. Some victims hate sex because physical intimacy in marriage triggers old feelings of abuse. It's difficult for many to enjoy the physical aspect of a marriage. They feel inhibited and have a hard time trusting their partner and letting go of the past. They fear sexual pleasure in their lives because it makes them feel guilty and ashamed. It can be like reliving the abuse all over again. On the other hand, some victims react quite differently. They develop a pattern of sexual promiscuity. They bring sex into relationships because they feel this is one way to get attention and affection. They are confused about true love and intimacy. Deep down inside, they want love and affection, but have learned to try to get it in the wrong way. They may have no conscious realization their sexual behavior is related to their past abuse. They repeat this pattern over and over again, jumping in and out of relationships and losing their sense of self-respect along the way.

Sexual abuse affects people in different ways. Todd's history of childhood sexual abuse played a major role in the development of his addiction to pornography. Despite a loving family, he kept his dark secret for a very long time. This impacted his psychological development in a negative way. He was traumatized by the abuse. Sexual abuse affects people in different ways. Not all victims of abuse engage in self-destructive patterns like Todd. Some victims of abuse manage to survive their ordeal without trauma such as depression and suicide. For many, however, the impact of abuse is devastating and life-changing.

Todd became depressed and suicidal. He felt ashamed, fearful of his parents' reaction if he disclosed the truth, and fearful of the offender's reaction to breaking the silence. Todd blamed himself for the abuse even though he was only a child and it wasn't his fault. He developed low self-esteem and confidence, feelings of insecurity and inadequacy as a male, as well as social anxiety. All these dynamics made him fragile and vulnerable to the use of pornography. The computer and the Internet became Todd's refuge, a temporary way to escape his inner pain. The more he withdrew from healthy social relationships, the more he depended on the Internet.

When Todd discovered pornography, he was immediately aroused and excited. One picture led to two pictures, and over time, a pattern developed where he became addicted to pornography. He felt ashamed of this behavior, but because he was so lonely most of the time, he began to justify his actions. This justification led to greater usage, and he found himself trapped in this dark world. The more time he spent trying to find some pleasure through sexual arousal, the more depressed he became. The more depressed he became, the more he withdrew from healthy relationships. His pornography usage escalated. It was a vicious cycle, one from which he could not escape.

When Todd first talked to a girl online, even though she was a minor, he felt a sense of social connection he was not achieving at school or through other types of social activities. He became a loner. The computer provided a barrier of safety. He didn't have to worry about rejection due to physical appearance. He was talking to someone and she was actually talking back. Given his neediness, this type of interaction made him feel better. He began to look forward to talking with this girl every day. That's all he thought about while at school. He wanted to get home as fast as he could, check to see if she wrote any emails, and ended up chatting with her into the late hours of the night. His school-work suffered. He was tired a lot. He lied to his parents, stating he was up late working on school projects. Despite knowing this girl was a minor, he began to care for her. He was developing a "virtual" relationship. As she shared personal information, he believed she cared for him. He began to form a mental picture of her although he had never seen her. He became attracted to her.

In the back of Todd's mind he knew she might not be the girl of his dreams; but his need for social connection was so strong he tried to block this out of his mind. As his confidence in the relationship grew, exchanging pictures over the Inter-net fueled his desire for her. He began to obsess about her and dreamed of a future together. Once his fear of rejection subsided, more pictures were exchanged. This was a big moment for Todd. She still liked him afterwards, and he cherished the pictures she sent him. He taped her picture to his computer monitor every time he talked with her.

Exchanging pictures led to the next step of wanting to hear her voice and chat on the phone. She gave Todd her phone number and he called her. Once he was comfortable talking on the phone, the desire to meet and see each other was the next natural step in their relationship. The more the fantasized relationship developed, the less Todd thought about her being a minor. His desire for affection and attention was stronger than the reality of any social or legal consequences. Once Todd decided to meet her, he blocked out any fear related to con-sequence. It didn't seem to matter; he'd found someone with whom he could bond emotionally.

When Todd was confronted and arrested by the police, he was scared to death. His fantasy world came crashing down. Todd was a good young man who really meant no harm to this girl. From his childhood abuse to his addiction to pornography, his life was spiraling downward for a very long time. Getting caught was actually a blessing in disguise. One example of this was that Todd had to go to counseling. This led to disclosing his abuse to his parents, confronting his offender face to face, and eventually developing social confidence and esteem.

The healing process takes time. Todd has made great strides in his personal growth. He has broken the bonds of pornography addiction and completed college, found a job, and developed a steady relationship with a girlfriend his age. Even though his story has a sad side to it, it's also a story about hope and renewal. One can overcome the impact of childhood sexual abuse. We see this every day in counseling. The road may be a challenging one, but many have the courage to cross the finish line. Fortunately, many resources exist to help this process.

Common Effects of Untreated Sexual Abuse

Sexual abuse affects victims in different ways. Some victims recover more rapidly than others and go on to live healthy and productive lives. For others, however, untreated symptoms of abuse persist into adulthood. According to The National Center for Post Traumatic Stress Disorders[1], victims of abuse frequently experience the following problems:

- Post-traumatic stress disorder or anxiety
- Depression and thoughts of suicide
- Sexual anxiety and disorders
- Poor body image and low self-esteem
- Unhealthy behaviors, such as alcohol abuse, drug abuse, self-mutilation, or binging and purging

Warning Signs of Child Sexual Abuse

The world has become an increasingly dangerous place for our children. We want to protect and keep them safe. No parent likes to think about sexual abuse. However, abuse is a real issue, and arming yourself with knowledge about the common warning signs of sexual abuse can help you keep them safe.

The Safe Child Program[2] defines sexual abuse as:

"… any sexual contact with a child or the use of a child for the sexual pleasure of someone else. This may include exposing private parts to the child or asking the child to expose him or herself, fondling of the genitals or requests for the child to do so, oral sex or attempts to enter the vagina or anus with fingers,

Common Fears about Reporting the Abuse

There are many reasons why victims of sexual abuse keep it a secret. Some of the most common reasons shared by male and female victims during counseling are:

- It's my fault.
- I'll get into some type of trouble.
- No one will believe me.
- My mom will be mad when he (dad or step dad) leaves.
- I'm confused; I don't know what to do.
- I feel ashamed and guilty.
- The offender might go to jail, and I still care about him.
- He won't like me anymore.
- He said he'd hurt me or someone in my family if I tell.

objects or penis, although actual penetration is rarely achieved."

There are a number of warning signs that a child may have been sexually abused. These include:

Physical Indicators

- Difficulty walking or sitting
- Torn clothing
- Stained or bloody underwear
- Pain or itching in genital area
- Venereal disease, especially in preteens
- Pregnancy

- I don't want to have to tell this story to strangers over and over again.
- I'm scared.
- I didn't make it stop.
- I'm too depressed to talk about it.
- I don't want to think about it. I'm trying to block it out of my mind.
- Kids at school will find out.
- They will call me gay.
- I'm afraid I'll have to testify in court.
- My parents won't trust me to go anywhere on my own again.
- My friends might shun me, hate me, or spread rumors about me.

You are no longer a victim. You have the power, control, and right to say whatever you want.

Hold onto the letter for a day or two, or for as long as you want. Then rip it up. Destroy it. Get rid of it. This is a symbolic gesture that the abuse is over and you will no longer be held captive to it. Many people feel better getting their feelings out in this way. It might be helpful to you if you still struggle with some aspect of the abuse.

A Letter Sent

This intervention is very similar to the one above. It's more confrontational, and sometimes victims feel uncomfortable taking this step. It's more risky if you're unsure how the offender may react. Some may get angry. Some may be very understanding. Often, people are more careful with what they say or how they say it. They are more restrained. You have to do what's right for you. If sending a letter feels uncomfortable or unsafe, then it's probably better not to send it.

A Phone Call

Talking to one's offender on the phone is a more direct form of communication. Some like this approach while others feel too intimidated and do not want to hear the offender's voice. This is more personal, but again, one cannot always predict how the offender will react. Some write down what they want to say because it's easier. Anxiety is common when taking this step. The bottom line: if you feel unsafe or highly anxious, this step is probably not for you.

Face-to-Face Contact

This step involves talking to the offender and expressing one's self directly. Most victims pick a place to meet where they feel safe. This can include a public place. Some take a support person along. They can sit in on the conversation or wait in the car. Whatever the victim feels right about doing should be done. Safety is always the first priority. It's difficult to talk to someone directly about abuse if they are the offender. This is a very difficult step for many to take, and usually completed only after the victim has gone to counseling, and the counselor has helped prepare the victim for such an encounter.

An Invitation to Counseling

Inviting the offender to counseling can be a very rewarding and healing experience. However, most offenders are resistant to this invitation. The counselor helps establish safety within the confines of the therapy office and decides with the victim the purpose and goals of the session. By letter or phone call, the offender is typically invited to a counseling session by the victim. A phone call can occur from the counselor's office. The counselor can also play a role in constructing the letter. Even if the offender rejects the invitation, a progressive step has occurred because it takes courage to take this type of step in the first place. It's a form of empowerment.

A WORD FROM TODD'S MOM

When my husband and I first found out Todd had been arrested, we were shocked and dumbfounded. We did not raise our son to get in trouble with the law. We were hurt, angry, confused, sad, and scared. We knew Todd had always had some struggles socially, but we hoped he would just grow out of it. We had no clue he had been sexually abused.

I cried for days when he first told us. I could not sleep, and I just kept picturing him getting abused. This all seemed like a bad dream. We could not understand why he never told us what happened. I've always been overly protective and I couldn't fathom how it had happened right under my nose. Moreover, I couldn't understand why anyone would want to hurt him like that.

I did not realize how frightened he was of his offender and how his fear and shame affected him so deeply. I also had no clue as to the potential dangers of the Internet, especially all the pornography out there. It is very frightening to think how many kids are involved in this type of problem without parents knowing what's going on.

I'm glad Todd's secret about his abusive past and pornography addiction is now out in the open. He went to counseling and has made a lot of progress. I know it's been a painful process for him— for us as well—but he's done a lot of growing up over the past few years. He had strayed from church, but now attends regularly. And his girlfriend seems really nice and supportive of him. Suicidal thinking, abuse, addiction, and legal trouble: these are a parent's worst nightmare. But now there is hope where there was once despair. That's something to be thankful for.

- -

A LETTER
FROM TODD'S COUNSELOR

Todd was referred to me for counseling by his attorney. I've worked with Todd for over three years and have gotten to know him quite well. At the onset of counseling, Todd was quiet and soft-spoken. It was difficult for him to talk openly about his thoughts and feelings. He was very suspicious and mistrustful. He suffered from low self-esteem and self-confidence. It was obvious Todd did not like himself very much. As Todd began to trust me more, he felt safe enough to share his life story. This was both a painful yet rewarding journey of self-discovery. Todd revealed he had a secret he'd safeguarded for years. He'd never told anyone this secret.

One day, Todd disclosed that he was sexually abused by a baby-sitter when he was a child. He told his story over a period of months, sharing only what he felt comfortable sharing during any given session. He described in vivid detail how he was abused. He was haunted by memories he could not get out of his head. Sometimes he cried and at other times he became angry. He blamed himself and questioned why he was targeted for abuse. He was also angry with himself. He felt he should have made the abuse stop. He felt he should have been strong and tough. He felt he had done something to encourage the offender.

Todd has made significant progress in changing his view of the abuse. He realizes he was a child and the abuse was not his fault. This was a big therapeutic step. He still gets angry with the offender and sometimes thinks of the abuse. But he also understands this is a normal part of the healing process.

Todd wrote a letter to his offender. This took months to complete. For so long he'd kept silent; he wasn't sure what to write. He crafted a letter expressing his anger. He read the letter out loud during a counseling session. After feeling some anger, and crying a tear, he ripped up the letter. This was to symbolize he was no longer a prisoner of abuse. He felt he had confronted his offender, letting out feelings that needed to be vented. He took some power back.

Todd is still my client. I'm very proud of the progress he's made. He's developed into a fine young man. His journey has been long and difficult, but well worth it.

Some men are curious about child pornography but are not motivated by sexual desires for children. However, if curiosity is accompanied by some sexual arousal, even if the arousal is minimal at first, the risk of developing a growing desire for child pornography increases.

For many men, looking at adult pornography puts them in a sexually charged or aroused state, physically and mentally. If child pornography is viewed during this time, then pleasure is once again associated with child pornography. The desire to look again is then reinforced unless the individual quickly turns away from the pornography, thus stopping the arousal before it becomes stronger. It's a form of conditioning. Pleasure is a powerful dynamic and type of reinforcement. Morals against looking at child pornography begin to fade, and the individual often rationalizes his behavior. What may start out as curiosity begins to evolve into a pattern of desire reinforced by looking at child pornography and experiencing pleasure.

An individual can obtain online child pornography and get into legal trouble in many ways, including:

- Trading child pornography to an undercover federal agent or police officer
- Trading child pornography to someone he believes is trustworthy, but who then reports him to the authorities
- Purchasing online child pornographic material from undercover federal authorities
- Buying child pornography from a manufacturer or distributor who is later arrested and whose distributor's list leads the authorities to him
- Trading pornography openly on the Internet through shareware and trading groups, which can be infiltrated by the authorities

The Legal Implications of Child Pornography

The possession of child pornography is illegal. This includes pornographic pictures or movies saved or stored on one's computer hard drive or onto computer discs.

Many incorrectly assume that deleting this material after looking at it erases it from the computer. Actually, the material is still saved on the computer's hard drive. The authorities have sophisticated software that recaptures the pictures believed to have been deleted. Imagine the shock and surprise some experience when pictures begin showing up on their computer's monitor during an investigation. Once these pictures appear, they can be used as evidence resulting in criminal charges under state and federal laws.

Frank Stanley is an experienced criminal defense lawyer in Grand Rapids, Michigan, who, among other things, specializes in the defense of individuals charged by federal or state authorities with any type of involvement with child pornography.[2] He shares his legal expertise below to help you better understand the potential legal ramifications of possessing child pornography.

Defining the Crime

Laws governing the investigation and prosecution of child pornography vary from state to state, but looking at Michigan's law will help illustrate the point that breaking these laws is a serious matter.

In Michigan, child pornography is called "child sexually abusive material." A *child* is defined as "a person who is less than eighteen years of age." This creates an interesting anomaly in that Michigan's age of consent is sixteen. In Michigan, it would be legally permissible to have consensual sex with a sixteen-year-old but legally impermissible to photograph or record the sexual act.

The Prevalence of Child Pornography on the Internet[1]

▪ Demand for pornographic images of babies and toddlers on the Internet is soaring. Moreover, the images are becoming more graphically violent and disturbing.

▪ The typical age of children is between six and twelve, but that profile is getting younger.

▪ Approximately twenty new children appear on porn sites every month, many of them kidnapped or sold into the pornography industry.

▪ More than 20,000 images of child pornography are posted on the Internet every week.

▪ According to researchers who monitored the Internet over a six-week period, more than 140,000 pornographic images of children were posted. Twenty children appearing in these images were estimated to have been abused for the first time, and more than 1,000 images of each child were created.

▪ Child pornography generates $3 billion annually.

Child sexually abusive material is defined as "a child engaging in a listed sexual act." *Listed sexual act* is defined as "sexual intercourse, erotic fondling, sadomasochistic abuse, masturbation, passive sexual involvement, sexual excitement, or erotic nudity."

Erotic fondling is defined as "touching a person's clothed or unclothed genitals, pubic area, buttocks, or, if the person is a female, breasts, or if the person is a child, the developing or undeveloped breast area, for the purpose of real or simulated overt sexual gratification or stimulation." Physical contact that is not for the purpose of sexual gratification or stimulation is expressly excluded from the definition.

Passive sexual involvement is defined as "a real or simulated act that is designed to expose another person to or draws another person's attention to one of the listed acts for the purpose of real or simulated overt sexual gratification or stimulation."

Erotic nudity is defined as "the lascivious exhibition of genital, pubic, or rectal area of any individual." *Lascivious* is in turn defined as "wanton, lewd, lustful, and tending to produce voluptuous or lewd emotion."

Federal Law

Federal law also criminalizes child pornography along with other specific crimes involving children, for example, interstate transportation of a child for an illicit purpose. Because Michigan and the federal government are two separate sovereigns, either or both jurisdictions could prosecute a person who violates the statute.

The definitional section under federal law speaks in terms of a depiction of "a minor engaging in sexually explicit conduct."

A *minor* is defined as "any person under the age of eighteen." However, different states may have different ages of consent for females and males.

Child pornography is defined as "any visual depiction, including any photograph, film, video, picture, or computer, or computer-generated image or picture, whether made or produced by electronic, mechanical, or other means of sexually explicit conduct."

Sexually explicit conduct is defined as including "graphic sexual intercourse of whatever type and whatever gender of the participants." This definition includes lascivious simulated sexual intercourse where the genitals, breast, or pubic area of any individual is exhibited. It also includes graphic depictions of lascivious simulated bestiality, masturbation, or sadistic or masochistic abuse and/or the graphic or simulated exhibition of the genitals or pubic area of any person.

Graphic means that "a viewer can observe any part of the genitals or pubic area of any depicted person, during any part of the time that sexually explicit conduct is being depicted."

Visual depiction is defined as including "undeveloped film and videotape, and the data stored on the computer disc or by electronic means which is capable of conversion into a visual image."

Once the authorities determine whether a picture on one's computer qualifies as child pornography, a decision is made as to whether or not the individual has committed a crime. For example, Michigan identifies three tiers of conduct. Each tier is subject to a different penalty. Each tier requires the person to "know, have reason to know, or should be reasonably expected to know" that the depiction is a depiction of a child. A person who does not take reasonable precautions to determine the age of someone depicted can be criminally implicated even if that person did not think the image depicted a child.

Tier One: The first tier includes anyone who "persuades, induces, entices, coerces, causes, or knowingly allows a child to engage in child sexually abusive activity for the purpose of producing any child sexually abusive material." This is commonly understood to be someone who has direct contact with the child whose images are being recorded. One published Michigan case involved one minor photographing two other minors having sex with one another.

The statute also includes in the first tier "a person who arranges for, produces, makes, or finances, or a person who attempts, prepares or conspires to arrange for, produce, make, or finance any child sexually abusive activity or child sexually abusive material."

A recent Michigan Court of Appeals case held that someone that would otherwise be a simple possessor (Tier 3) could be prosecuted as a Tier 1 violator. In that case, the individual downloaded images from the Internet onto CDRs. The CDRs were not disseminated to anyone else. They were intended as a means of storage. Nevertheless, because the individual had copied the images onto the CDRs, the Court considered him to be a producer. This was deemed true even though the individual had never had contact with the child depicted and didn't know the child's identity.

Tier Two: The second tier includes a person who "distributes, promotes or finances the distribution or promotion or receives for the purposes of distribution or promotion, or conspires, attempts, or prepares to distribute, receive, finance, or promote any child sexually abusive material." This tier has historically included individuals who disseminate the images to others. This tier could include the original creators of the pornography. It also could include those individuals who obtain the images from whatever sources and distribute them to others. It also includes people that finance the distribution operation.

Tier Three: The third tier includes a person who knowingly possesses any child sexually abusive material. This tier has historically included the end-user, that is, an individual who possesses the material for personal reasons who had nothing to do with the original creation of the material and who does not disseminate the material to any third party.

Consequences: Federal or State Prison

Both Michigan and the federal government use sentencing guidelines to compute a sentencing range. The Michigan guidelines are presently mandatory. The federal guidelines are supposedly advisory, but they are quasi-mandatory since most sentences are imposed within those guidelines. The federal penalties are much more severe than the Michigan penalties. In a recent example, an individual who was convicted by a federal court for possession of child pornography received a 14 year sentence. Had that individual been prosecuted in a Michigan state court, the minimum sentence would have been approximately 3 years.

It is a sobering moment in the lives of many offenders. Defendants often have no real idea or clue as to the seriousness of their crime in the eyes of the community and court. If a law is broken, the court must respond accordingly. Hearing the judge's proclamation of "Mr. Smith, you are hereby sentenced to the Jackson Correctional Facility for a period of three to five years" is a powerful dose of reality.

Criminal Penalties

Mr. Stanley outlines the potential legal consequences or penalties associated with child pornography. These penalties may differ depending on the state where the crime is committed. Regardless, these consequences are real and life changing.

Both Michigan and the federal government use sentencing guidelines to compute a sentencing range. The Michigan guidelines are presently mandatory. The federal guidelines are supposedly advisory, but they are quasi-mandatory since most sentences are imposed within those guidelines. A defendant can be charged at both the state and federal level. There are many factors that can influence the penalty assigned to the crime, for example, physical injury to victim, psychological injury to victim, number of victims, criminal sexual penetration, and defendant's criminal history. A very long prison sentence (more than twenty years) is also a possibility under federal guidelines.

In Michigan law, the statutory maximum penalties are:

TIER 1	not more than twenty years
TIER 2	not more than seven years
TIER 3	not more than four years
TIER 1 and computers	not more than twenty years
TIER 2 and computers	not more than ten years
TIER 3 and computers	not more than seven years

In federal law, the defendant is not eligible for parole and will likely serve the sentence imposed, less an allowance for good time. The good time allowance is presently 15% of a person's sentence. Good time is not automatic. It must be earned by good behavior.

In Michigan law, a minimum and a maximum sentence is imposed. The maximum sentence is set by statute. The minimum sentence is set by the Court. The minimum sentence is a parole eligibility date. However, eligibility is not the same as entitlement, and many Michigan prisoners serve well beyond their minimum dates.

Scriptural Guidance
for Keeping Your Balance

There is a clear distinction between legal pornography and child pornography, which has profound legal consequences. Unfortunately, many men fail to notice they are getting dangerously close to the edge of legality. It is as if they are dancing on the edge of a cliff. And if they do not exercise control and restraint, they risk plummeting to the valley of serious legal and personal consequences.

For those men, inspiration can be found in the following episode of the life of the prophet Ezekiel:

> *The hand of the Lord was upon me, and he brought me out by the Spirit of the Lord and set me in the middle of a valley; it was full of bones. He led me back and forth among them, and I saw a great many bones on the floor of the valley, bones that were very dry. He asked me, "Son of man, can these bones live?"*
>
> *I said, "O Sovereign Lord, you alone know."*
>
> *Then he said to me, "Prophesy to these bones and say to them, 'Dry bones, hear the word of the Lord. This is what the Sovereign Lord says to these bones: I will make breath enter you, and you will come to life. I will attach*

tendons to you and make flesh come upon you and cover
you with skin; I will put breath in you, and you will come
to life. Then you will know that I am the Lord."

So I prophesied as I was commanded. And as I was
prophesying, there was a noise, a rattling sound, and the
bones came together, bone to bone. I looked, and tendons
and flesh appeared on them and skin covered them, but
there was no breath in them.

Then he said to me, "Prophesy to the breath; proph-
esy, son of man, and say to it, 'This is what the Sover-
eign Lord says: Come from the four winds, O breath, and
breathe into these slain, that they may live.'" So I prophe-
sied as he commanded me, and breath entered them; they
came to life and stood up on their feet—a vast army.

Then he said to me: "Son of man, these bones are the
whole house of Israel. They say, 'Our bones are dried up
and our hope is gone; we are cut off.' Therefore, prophesy
and say to them, 'This is what the Sovereign Lord says: O
my people, I am going to open your graves and bring you
up from them; I will bring you back to the land of Israel.
Then you, my people, will know that I am the Lord, when
I open your graves and bring you up from them. I will put
my Spirit in you and you will live, and I will settle you in
your own land. Then you will know that I, the Lord, have
spoken, and I have done it, declares the Lord.'"

EZEKIEL 37:1–14, NIV

There is tremendous hope to be found in this text from the prophecy of Ezekiel. The context is the Babylonian captivity; the ancient Israelites were being held captive in Babylon. With their situation seeming to be hopeless, the people lamented, *"Our bones are dried up and our hope is gone."* But God orders the prophet Ezekiel to prophesy to the bones and tell them they are going to live again. The Lord God said, *"I am going to open your graves and bring you up from them; I will bring you back to the land of Israel."*

That was an important message to the people of Israel, a people held in captivity in Babylon. And it is an important message for those who have been held captive by a life of cyber-sex and pornography. This is a message of hope and renewal for those who look around their lives and see only decay and believe, like the Israelites, their situation is hopeless.

Prior to the Babylonian captivity, Israel had been stubborn and disobedient, bowing down and worshipping other gods. As punishment, God allowed Israel to be taken captive to Babylon, which became a "graveyard" for the people. At times their conditions were bearable, but most often they were oppressed. They couldn't build their life in the foreign land and they couldn't go home. After twenty years away from home, the Israelites began to lose hope. They started asking some fundamental questions like, *Where is God? Why hasn't God delivered us? Why is this happening to us?*

According to Psalm 137, the people were so distraught; they couldn't even sing the songs of their faith that they loved so much. They had hung up their harps and sat bitter and despondent by the banks of the river Chebar. They had lost their land of promise and were unable to experience God's presence. They felt spiritually dead. They felt alone and abandoned.

Perhaps, like the ancient Israelites, you feel spiritually dead. Perhaps you wonder if you can even consider yourself a Christian anymore. You find yourself unable to pray, unable to sing, unable to hope.

Not unlike the ancient Israelites, your spouse also knows what it's like to feel abandoned. Her life has been shattered by your Internet infidelity. She has discovered the extent to which you have been held captive by the dark forces of pornography, and she feels rejected. Your promises to her have been broken,

Predators want kids to believe they've found a trusted friend who understands them like their parents cannot. They've often had extensive experience talking with children, and the anonymity of the Internet emboldens them and reinforces their fantasies. They can hide in the darkness of cyberspace. So don't be fooled into thinking that just because you can't see them, they're not out there.

They are prowling around on the Internet in places kids frequent, looking to make a connection with a child, and they know it's only a matter of time before they'll be successful. If they're lucky, they'll even convince him or her to meet offline. What happens next often makes the news, and the details can be frightening.

Such predators have always known where kids congregate, and now the Internet has opened up a new "playground" for them to frequent. They pass themselves off as teenagers and young adults. Some, trying a more "honest" approach, admit they are grown men and act as supportive father figures to win over a child's trust. One should never underestimate the ability

Safety Tips for Kids

Please review these safeguards with your children.

- Never give out personal information about yourself or family (name, address, phone number, email address, or passwords to blogs).

- Never give a stranger a photo of yourself. Let your friends know not to pass out your pictures either. Once a photo is sent out over the Internet, you can never get it back. It can be traded and passed on to others hundreds of times. Remember, a picture identifies who you are. Some predators, having gotten a hold of pictures and general locations of children, have sought them out—sometimes successfully.

of the predator to gain access to kids. They spend a lot of time analyzing and developing different approaches.

Parents need to understand and accept that the Internet can be a very dangerous place. However, they are not helpless to protect their children. They can and should educate themselves, establish some family rules for using the Internet, and start a dialogue with their kids about the very real dangers lurking in cyberspace.

Talking about this subject with your children—especially if they're teenagers—can be difficult. They may believe and act like they know everything. But they don't have the life experience you do, and they still need and depend on you despite their push for independence. It's important to communicate that your reason for the discussion is because you love them and want to protect them. They may still tune you out or argue about any rules you try to implement. But in time they will realize you backed up your declarations of "I love you" with actions.

Being a parent isn't easy. You may have to overcome some of your own fears in order to broach this subject with your kids.

- Never meet people you've met through the Internet offline. Never! You may think you know them, but you have no idea whether the person they've portrayed themselves to be is who they really are. People lie about age, sex, and other personal factors all the time.

- Never accept emails, pictures, or instant messages from strangers.

- Tell a parent if someone online tries to engage you in sexual chat. Cyber-crime can and should be reported to the police.

- If a friend is threatened or harassed online or tells you she plans on meeting someone offline, tell your parents and hers immediately. Your friend may be upset with you, but that phone call may save her life.

safe to go online. In the middle of a sexual conversation with a man, I had a pornographic image of a woman enlarged on my computer screen. My wife walked into the bedroom and caught me masturbating. She was shocked and angry. We had a long talk that night and I broke down and told her of my struggles with pornography.

When she calmed down, she suggested I call our pastor the next day. I called him first thing in the morning and met him to discuss this issue. He recognized I had a sexual addiction problem and referred me to a specialist who treated these problems. It was a very, very embarrassing meeting, but I disclosed the truth. I wound up going to counseling and a 12-step support group for sexual addicts. It was a turning point in my life. I made a commitment to get this problem under control. It has been a challenging road to recovery, and although there have been times when I have slipped up and looked at pornography again, I worked hard to get the problem under control. My life was chaos and I was drifting more into the dark side of sexual addiction. Thank goodness my pastor was willing to talk to me openly about my problem and help me get back on the right path.

The Chaos of Sexual Addiction

Larry is a sex addict. This means he developed a psychological dependency on sex e.g. Internet pornography. Larry's case is important to understand because it demonstrates how curiosity about pornography can escalate into an addictive pattern and become a destructive habit over time. Some become addicted within weeks while others progress over months. Everyone's pattern is unique to the individual.

Larry was once an innocent little boy who knew nothing about sexuality and the dangers of pornography. The seeds of his addiction were unknowingly planted by his father. He discovered by accident his father's pornography. Imagine how Larry's life journey might have been different if his father had not used pornography.

Instead of keeping his youthful innocence, Larry began to crave pornography and the feelings of arousal and pleasure associated with it. Like alcoholics crave their drug, Larry craved pornography.

Larry was socially insecure as a child and teen. Pornography filled a void in his life. It made him feel good. It helped him cope with social anxiety and the fear of rejection. He used sex to cope with problems and stress in his adult life. Like many addicts, pornography became his crutch. It was his shameful secret.

Larry's addiction continued after marriage. For many addicts, they hope marriage will be the solution to this problem because of the availability of sex. Sometimes this can help, and the addiction lays dormant for a while. In other cases, the addict "brings the addiction" into the marriage and learns to hide it from their spouse rather than confront the problem.

Larry was afraid of exposing his secret life. He feared social criticism and judgment. He hid behind the anonymity of the computer. When he became bored with pornography, he found chatrooms. This was an exciting discovery. He justified his actions and his addiction escalated. When caught by his wife, the walls hiding his addiction came tumbling down. The secret was out of the bag. It was time to look into the mirror and face reality.

Larry's story is also one of strength and courage. It takes courage to admit when one has a problem and face it directly. He was willing to share his story with others. Larry went to counseling, found a twelve step-recovery support group and sought spiritual guidance from his pastor. These were necessary steps for recovery to take place. He took the first step by admitting he had a problem. This courageous first step led to a journey of exploration and healing. Larry's new motto: "No more secrets."

The Cycle of Sexual Addiction

Patrick Carnes played an instrumental role in advocating for the concept of sexual addiction as a recognizable and treatable problem. He authored the book entitled *Out of the Shadows* in the 1980s, which discussed sexual addiction.[2] He went on to author additional books which helped to explain the complexities of sexual addiction.

Carnes believed that sex could become an addiction for some people, just as drugs and alcohol become an addiction for other people. Like other addictions, sexual addiction bears four hallmarks: It builds tolerance. It produces withdrawal. It follows obsessive-compulsive patterns. And finally, sexual addiction produces shame.

Moreover, Carnes determined six warning signs for people to look for in order to determine whether sex has become

What Is Sexual Addiction?

Several conceptual models have been developed to understand sexual addiction. Mark Griffiths[1] identified six core components of addiction, including:

Salience. *Salience* occurs when Internet sex becomes the most important activity in the person's life and dominates their thinking (preoccupations and cognitive distortions), feelings (cravings), and behavior (deterioration of socialized behavior). For instance, even if the person is not actually on their computer engaged in Internet sex they will be thinking about the next time they will be.

Mood modification. *Mood modification* refers to the subjective experience (an arousing "buzz" or "high" or paradoxically tranquilizing feeling of "escape" or "numbing") that people report having as a consequence of engaging in Internet sex. It is often viewed as coping strategy.

Tolerance. *Tolerance* is the process whereby increasing amounts of Internet sex are required to achieve the former mood an addiction. Addictive sex is done in isolation. Addictive sex is secretive. It is devoid of intimacy. It is devoid of relationship. It is victimizing. And addictive sex always ends in despair.

As Carnes studied sexual addiction, he noted that it progressed through four levels. In level one, the addict uses fantasy, pornography, and masturbation to achieve a high (that is, sexual release). In level two, the addict needs live pornography to provide release. He also may develop a fetish and seek sex outside of marriage to feed his high.

By level three, the addict's growing drive may lead to minor criminal offenses, prostitution, voyeurism, and/or exhibitionism. If he does not seek help at this point for his addiction, he

modifications effects. This basically means that for someone engaged in Internet sex, they gradually build up the amount of the time they spend on front of the computer engaged in the behavior.

Withdrawal. *Withdrawal* symptoms are the unpleasant feeling states and/or physical effects which occur when Internet sex is discontinued or suddenly reduced (e.g., the shakes, moodiness, irritability, etc.).

Conflict. *Conflict* refers to the conflicts between the Internet user and those around them (interpersonal conflict), conflicts with other activities (job, social life, hobbies, and interests), or conflicts within themselves (intrapsychic conflict and/or subjective feelings of loss of control), which are concerned with spending too much time engaged in Internet sex.

Relapse. *Relapse* is the tendency for repeated reversions to earlier patterns of Internet sex to recur and for even the most extreme patterns typical of the height of excessive Internet sex to be quickly restored after many years of abstinence or control.

In the first day of creation, God creates order out of chaos. He creates light to balance the darkness. And he creates time by establishing a predictable progression from darkness to light, from evening to morning. This simple fact of life on earth—– that the planet rotates regularly on its axis, that after every midnight there will be a dawn—gives order and stability to both our physical and spiritual existence. Every child who is frightened of the dark clings to this predictable truth. A Hebrew morning prayer praises God as "the One who renews creation every day." Each day's dawn renews our connection to the Creator and offers us the promise of a new beginning.[5]

Cybersexual addiction leads to personal and family chaos. There are very real consequences for straying from God's plan and purpose. When a person is addicted to sex, their entire spiritual life spins out of control. But there is hope. God continues to create order out of chaos.

Read through the verses written above from the book of Genesis. As you read, notice the pattern within the verses. Notice how the ancient writers used repetition to emphasize and punctuate the beauty of the process of creation. Notice how on each day of creation it is written, "And there was evening, and there was morning—the first day." And the second day. And the third and the fourth, the fifth, and the sixth. With each stage of creating order out of chaos it is proclaimed that it was a day, and that it was good. But notice the absence of such repetition for the seventh day.

Could it be that the ancient writers were helping us to understand that God continues to be involved in our world? That God continues to participate in your life? That God continues to work with you to help create order out of your chaos?

The story of creation does indeed demonstrate how God created order out of chaos. And that creative, redemptive power is still available to those who believe in Him.

Strategies for Recovery and Change

The first step in healing and recovery is to admit one has a problem. This can also be the most difficult step to take. Shame and embarrassment, lack of understanding and awareness of the destructive nature of cyber sexual behavior, and resistance to break the addiction pattern because of pleasure keep many from taking this important step toward change. Admission of a problem takes courage and builds character. It results in taking responsibility for ones actions. People are more likely to change when they recognize a problem and are motivated to fix it. The stronger the motivation the better.

Changing old habits or patterns which have been around for a long time is hard work. There can be self-doubt, a tendency to give up easily and fear of failure. It can be easy to give up in the face of adversity. It is often a daily battle and often times there are relapses. The craving to satisfy sexual desire is powerful and intoxicating. Fortunately, there is a way to attack this problem and win the battle. Larry's case illustrates the keys to victory.

Developing a Game Plan

Prayer

Larry was encouraged to pray on a daily basis for healing and spiritual renewal. This included praying every time he felt the desire to sexually act out. He was comforted to know he had a powerful weapon at his disposal. He learned prayer worked and began a prayer routine. He started and ended each day with prayer and personal reflection. This helped get the day off to a good start and relax before bedtime. It gave him confidence that he could face any temptation that would come his way.

a pornography Web site. Another option is to install software that blocks pornographic images altogether.

Larry followed the motto of taking one day at a time. Every good day counts as a victory. Every temptation that is resisted is a victory. There will be many temptations to relapse, but these are opportunities for change and success. Every desire to turn on the computer and look at pornography that is thwarted is a win. Each win is a building block toward personal growth and maturity. Over time, one's character will change in a positive way and the desire to use pornography will decrease.

Larry also attended a support group designed to assist men and women in recovery from sexual issues. He found the support of the group to be very helpful. He was able to learn from others experiences and realized he was not alone in his suffering. He was very nervous and embarrassed, but overcame his insecurities and shared openly about his struggles with pornography.

- -

A WORD FROM LARRY'S PASTOR

Larry came to me a broken man. When he told me he had a problem with Internet pornography, we immediately prayed for forgiveness and healing. I referred Larry to a counselor I knew who dealt with this kind of problem. His counselor confirmed Larry had an addiction to pornography and began to develop a treatment plan for him. I, along with a group of men from our church, became Larry's accountability and prayer partners. Together, we helped Larry refocus his spirituality. This proved invaluable to Larry's recovery.

Notes

Chapter 1

1. Alexa Research. (2001). *Alexa Research finds "sex" popular on web.* Business Wire, February 14, 2001.

2. Cooper, A., Delmonico, D., & Burg, R. (2000). Cybersex users, abusers, and compulsives: New findings and implications. In A. Cooper (Ed.), *Cybersex: The dark side of the force* (pp. 5-29). Philadelphia: Brunner-Routledge.

3. Focus on the Family. (2000). *Zogby survey reveals a growing percentage of those seeking sexual fulfillment on the Internet.* Retrieved March 1, 2003 from the World Wide Web: www.pureintimacy.org/news/a0000031.html

4. Schlosser, E. The Business of Pornography. U.S. News & World Report (Feb. 10, 1997): 42.

5. Cited in: *Archive of Statistics on Internet Dangers,* Enough Is Enough, Retrieved from the World Wide Web on October 26, 2008 at www.enough.org.

Chapter 2

1. MSNBC/Stanford/Duquesne Study, Washington Times, January 26, 2000.

2. Ibid.

3. Ropelato, Jerry (2007). *Internet Pornography Statistics.* Internet Filter Review. Retrieved from the Wold Wide Web on October 26, 2008 : http://internet-filter-review.toptenreviews.com/internet-pornography-statistics.html

4. Cooper, A., (2000). Cybersex users, abusers, and compulsives: New findings and implications. In A. Cooper (Ed.), *Cybersex: The dark side of the force* (pp. 5-29). Philadelphia: Brunner-Routledge.

5. Grundner, Tom ((2000). The Skinner Box Effect. Lincoln, Nebraska: Writers Club Press.

Chapter 3

1. Steketee, Gail; Pigott, Teresa; and Schemmel, Todd (2003). Obsessive Compulsive Disorder: The Latest Assessment and Treatment Strategies. Kansas City, MO: Compact Clinicals.

Chapter 4

1. Cooper, A., (2000). Cybersex users, abusers, and compulsives: New findings and implications. In A. Cooper (Ed.), *Cybersex: The dark side of the force* (pp. 5-29). Philadelphia: Brunner-Routledge.

2. Schneider, J. P. (2000). Effects of cybersex addiction on the family: Results from a survey. In A. Cooper (Ed.), *Cybersex: The Dark Side of the Force* (pp. 31-58). Philadelphia: Brunner-Routledge.

3. Quittner, J. (April 14, 1997). Divorce Internet style. *Time*, 72.

4. Smedes, Lewis (1984). Forgive and Forget: Healing the Wounds We Don't Deserve. San Francisco, CA: Harper San Francisco.

5. Ibid.

6. Flanigan, Beverly (1992). Forgiving the Unforgivable: Uncovering The Bitter Legacy of Intimate Wounds. New York: Collier Books.

7. Adapted from Flanigan's model of reciprocal forgiveness and reconciliation.

8. National Institute of Mental Health (2007). *Depression.* Retrieved from the World Wide Web on August 15, 2007: http://www.nimh.nih.gov/healthinformation/depressionmenu.cfm

Chapter 5

1. Sharf, Richard S. (1996). Theories of Psychotherapy and Counseling: Concepts and Cases. Pacific Grove, CA: Brooks/Cole Publishing Company.

2. Cooper, A., Delmonico, D., & Burg, R. (2000). Cybersex users, abusers, and compulsives: New findings and implications. In A. Cooper (Ed.), *Cybersex: The dark side of the force* (pp. 5-29). Philadelphia: Brunner-Routledge.

3. Schneider, J. P. (2000). Effects of cybersex addiction on the family: Results from a survey. In A. Cooper (Ed.), *Cybersex: The Dark Side of the Force* (pp. 31-58). Philadelphia: Brunner-Routledge.

4. Ibid: Sharf, Richard S.

Chapter 7

1. Whealin, J. (n.d.). Child Sexual Abuse. National Center for PTSD Fact Sheet. Retrieved from the World Wide Web on March 26, 2006: http://www.ncptsd.va.gov/ncmain/ncdocs/fact_shts/fs_child_sexual_abuse.html?opm=1&rr=rr1747&srt=d&echorr=true

2. Kraizer, S. (1996). Sexual Abuse. The Safe Child Program. Retrieved from the World Wide Web on March 21, 2006: http://safechild.org/childabuse1.htm#Indicators%20of%20Sexually%20Abusive%20Parent/Guardian

3. Darkness to Light (2007) *Statistics Surrounding Child Sexual Abuse*. Retrieved from the World Wide Web on August 27, 2007: www.darkness2light.org/KnowAbout

Chapter 8

1. Frank Stanley can be contacted at: Frank Stanley, P.C., Attorney At Law, 200 North Division Avenue, Grand Rapids, Michigan 48503

Chapter 9

1. Operation Innocence Online (2008). Retrieved from the World Wide Web on October 26, 2008: http://innocenceonline.com/statistics-main.asp

Chapter 10

1. Griffiths, Mark (2000). *Does Internet and Computer "Addiction" Exist? Some Case Study Evidence*. Cyberpsychology & Behavior, 3(2): 211-218.

2. Carnes, P. (1983). *Out of the shadows: Understanding Sexual Addiction*. Minneapolis, Minn: Compcare.

3. For more information about these recovery support groups, go to: www.sa.org , www.sca-recovery.org, and www.slaafws.org

4. For more information go to: www.celebrationrecovery.com

5. Rosenblatt, Naomi, and Horwitz, Joshua. (1995). Wrestling With Angels. New York: Delacorte Press.